I CAN
CONQUER IT

Felicia,
My ride or die!
Keep rising to the top! Be Blessed!,
Donna M. Slatky
3/1/19

I CAN
CONQUER IT

DAILY AFFIRMATIONS
FOR CONQUERING LIFE'S ISSUES

Sweet Read
PUBLISHING

4617 PINEVIEW DR
WILMINGTON, NC 28412
sweetreadpublishing@gmail.com

You Can Conquer It!

Whatever you are facing in life, with God's help, you can conquer it!

"We are more than conquerors through Him that loved us"
Romans 8:37

I dedicate this book to my brother, Charles W. Stallings, II, who we affectionately called "Chuck." Unfortunately, while you were here on earth, I didn't fully understand your pain and what you were going through. However, I want you to know, I get it now. I'm so happy that you finally "Conquered It," and are resting in the arms of our Lord and Savior, Jesus Christ. Rest in Heaven, Chuck. Be Blessed!

DONNA M. STALLINGS was born and raised in Alexandria, Virginia, but left there in 1980 to attend college at Virginia Commonwealth University. After graduating in 1984, she decided to make Richmond her home. She started her career in the insurance industry, but after 15 years of working in various lines of insurance, she left corporate America to work in the nonprofit industry. She worked for five different nonprofits over the course of 18 years ranging from homeless services case management to homeownership program management. She currently works as a Grant Programs Specialist for the Virginia Housing Development Authority.

Donna M. Stallings
icanconquerit@gmail.com

Copyright © 2018 by Donna M. Stallings
ISBN-13: 978-0-9860941-3-2

All rights reserved. No portion of this book may be reproduced in any form or by any means, including electronic storage and retrieval systems, except by explicit prior written permission of the publisher.

Cover design by Louis Penn from VisualConceptionz
Editors: Sarah E. Bode, Sophie Appel, Theodore Burgh, Ann Burgh
Book layout by Sophie Appel

Printed in the United States of America

Sweet Read Publishing
4617 Pineview Dr.
Wilmington, NC 28412
www.sweetreadpublishing.com
sweetreadpublishing@gmail.com

JANUARY 1

Setting Goals

When you set a goal, you should post a picture of the goal so you can envision it coming into being. For example, if you are trying to purchase a home, you could put a picture of the type of home you are trying to buy in a place where you can look at it every day. This will help to keep you focused and disciplined because you are constantly being reminded of your goal and what it will be like once you achieve it. Conversely, it would not be a good idea to post an unflattering picture of yourself if you're trying to lose weight, because you will constantly be reminded of the current state you are in instead of the ideal size you want to be. Your vision should always reflect something positive. As you continue to walk in faith, you will not only see your goal as being attainable, you will also see it come into fruition! "For the vision is yet for an appointed time, but at the end it shall speak, and not lie: though it tarry, wait for it; because it will surely come, it will not tarry." Be Blessed!

Habakkuk 2:2-3

DAILY REFLECTIONS

JANUARY 2

God's Approval

If we want things to change in our lives, *we* have to be willing to change and do something different. However, it is not only hard for us to change old habits and behaviors, but it is also hard for those around us to accept the new person we've become. If we allowed people to mistreat us in the past, and we decide to put a stop to it—they're not going to be thrilled about it. In fact, they may even fight us on it! But remember, "[I]f any man be in Christ, he is a new creature: old things are passed away; behold, all things are become new." So, even if man does not approve of us, God's approval is the only one that matters. "Show me a sign of your evident goodwill and favor, Lord, that those who hate me may see it and be put to shame, because You, Lord, will show Your approval of me when You help and comfort me." Be Blessed!

2 Corinthians 5:17, Psalm 86:17 (Amplified Version)

DAILY REFLECTIONS

___
___
___
___
___
___
___
___

JANUARY 3

God's Word

In dealing with our everyday struggles, we must learn to apply God's Word to our lives. If we don't know the Word, we can't use it. If we don't believe the Word, we can't stand on it. If we don't pray the Word, there is no intercession. And if we don't speak or confess the Word, there is no deliverance! "How can a young man keep his way pure? By living according to Your Word. I seek you with all my heart; do not let me stray from your commands. I have hidden Your Word in my heart that I might not sin against you. Praise be to you, O Lord; teach me your decrees… Your Word is a lamp to my feet and a light for my path." Therefore, arm yourself with God's Word at all times, so you are able to use it whenever the enemy attacks! Be Blessed!

Psalm 119:9-12, 105

DAILY REFLECTIONS

JANUARY 4

Freedom in Christ

Did you know that some people are comfortable staying in bondage? They know they have issues and what they need to do in order to get well, but yet they stay stuck. Why? Because they would rather stay in the misery that they are familiar with, than face what they do not know. The fear of the unknown can be a crippling thing for some people and can imprison them in their mind. God has already assured us that He has given us the victory and deliverance is ours. The prison door of our mind has been opened; we just have to walk out. So, don't spend your life being imprisoned and walking in fear. "It is for freedom that Christ has set us free. Stand firm, then, and do not let yourselves be burdened again by a yoke of slavery." "Whom the Son sets free is free indeed." Be Blessed!

Galatians 5:1, John 8:36

DAILY REFLECTIONS

JANUARY 5

Strength

So many times when the enemy attacks, we try to fight him back in our own strength. The truth is, we're not that strong. We need God! "We can do all things through Christ who strengthens us." The Bible never says we can do it in our own strength. Therefore, stop getting beat up by the enemy because you're trying to do everything by yourself. This is not a physical battle, but a spiritual one, so you need the Holy Spirit to be victorious. "If God is for you, who can be against you?" "Thanks be to God! He gives us the victory through our Lord Jesus Christ." Be Blessed!

Philippians 4:13, Romans 8:31, 1 Corinthians 15:57

DAILY REFLECTIONS

JANUARY 6

Acceptance

People who are striving for perfection don't realize they are trying to reach a goal that is impossible. When God made everything and said that it was good, He never said it was without flaws. We all have flaws and imperfections. The good news is He loves us in spite of them. He made our flaws on purpose, because in doing so, whenever we succeed despite our flaws, God gets the glory. So, we shouldn't get discouraged because we're not perfect. No one is! Realize it is a blessing that God can use us in spite of our imperfections! "Christ is the one who made us acceptable to God. He made us pure and holy, and He gave Himself to purchase our freedom." So, let's accept our freedom in Christ, and lay aside that weight of perfectionism! Be Blessed!

1 Corinthians 1:26-30

DAILY REFLECTIONS

JANUARY 7

Casting Your Cares

As long as we're here on this earth, we'll have issues to deal with. It's how we deal with them that makes the difference. We can deal with them in the flesh and continue to be frustrated, or we can take them to God, and let His divine intervention prevail. Without God, we can do nothing, but with God, we can do all things. "I can do all things through Christ who strengthens me." Be Blessed!

Philippians 4:13

DAILY REFLECTIONS

JANUARY 8

Humility

God has a way of humbling us whenever we are tempted to become judgmental. It is easy to judge someone who has a habit that is not an issue for us. I remember how I used to get frustrated with family members who would not stop smoking. I didn't understand it, because smoking was not an issue for me. God had to humble me by asking, "What was I going to do about my overeating?" All of us struggle with something, whether it is smoking, drinking, drugs, gambling, gossiping, sex, overeating, etc. We *all* need Jesus! Once we realize that, we can stop looking down on those who have not yet received their deliverance; knowing that it is only because of the grace of God that we have been able to overcome our issues and walk in victory! And just as Christ saved us from our addictive behaviors, He can save them, too. "We believe it is through the grace of our Lord Jesus that we are saved, just as they are." Be Blessed!

Acts 15:11

DAILY REFLECTIONS

JANUARY 9

Patience

Sometimes when you must wait a long time for God's promises to come into fruition, you get tired and try to help Him along. However, you must remember, God doesn't need your help. Look at how Abram and Sarai interfered with God's plan, and potentially did more harm than good. Because "He is faithful that promised," He will bring it to pass at the proper time. "Therefore, my dear brothers, stand firm. Let nothing move you. Always give yourselves fully to the work of the Lord, because you know that your labor in the Lord is not in vain." Remember, if the Lord said it, you can count on it. He will do just what He said! **Be Blessed!**

Genesis 16, Hebrews 10:23, 1 Corinthians 15:58

DAILY REFLECTIONS

JANUARY 10

Victory

When the enemy comes at you hurling his fiery darts, remember that "no weapon formed against you shall prosper." You are a child of the King, and a "royal priesthood." Therefore, you don't have to run in fear, or become anxious or distraught. The Lord says, "Vengeance is mine," and He will vindicate you. So, take up your "sword of the spirit," which is God's Word, and move forward in victory, knowing that "the weapons of our warfare are not carnal, but mighty through God to the pulling down of strongholds." We might be in a battle, but the good news is, in the end, we win! Be Blessed!

Isaiah 54:17, Romans 12:19, Ephesians 6:17, 2 Corinthians 10:4

DAILY REFLECTIONS

Hearing God

Sometimes when you encounter situations in life that require a major decision, you need to get quiet and hear what God has to say about it. You don't have to try to do everything by yourself because God has instructed you to, "Trust in the Lord with all your heart and lean not on your own understanding; in all your ways acknowledge Him, and He will make your paths straight." He's standing right there waiting to help you, but you're not giving Him your ear. Remember, "the steps of a good man are ordered by the Lord," so stop trying to run everything and step back and let God take control! Be Blessed!

Proverbs 3:5-6, Psalm 37:23

DAILY REFLECTIONS

JANUARY 12

Doubt

So many times, we are tempted to give up on the promises of God because it takes so long for them to come into fruition. However, if we are children of God, quitting is not an option. God is never late, but He will never be early either. Instead, He is always right on time. So, when you feel like you're at the end of your rope, and you can't take it anymore, remember that "the race is not given to the swift or the battle to the strong, but he that endureth unto the end shall be saved." Be Blessed!

Ecclesiastes 9:11, Matthew 24:13

DAILY REFLECTIONS

_____
_____
_____
_____
_____
_____
_____
_____
_____
_____

JANUARY 13

Trusting God

If God said it, then that settles it! We often get caught up in how a circumstance may look. But "God is not a man that He should lie, nor a son of man that He should change His mind. Does He speak and then not act? Does He promise and not fulfill?" We can stand firm on His promise that He will do just what He said. "Know therefore that the Lord your God is God; He is the faithful God, keeping His covenant of love to a thousand generations of those who love Him and keep His commands." Be Blessed!

Numbers 23:19, Deuteronomy 7:9

DAILY REFLECTIONS

JANUARY 14

God's Help

Sometimes we can be too smart for our own good. So many of us try to analyze and figure out what God is doing in our lives. Unfortunately, God is not some algebra equation that we can plug a formula into and get a calculated answer. God is sovereign, and that means He can do whatever He wants to, whenever He wants to, and however He wants to. By the time we try to figure it out, God has already worked it out! So, let's stop wasting time trying to help God do His job and just concentrate on doing ours! "I lift up my eyes to the hills—where does my help come from? My help comes from the LORD." Notice when the question was asked about where our help comes from, the answer was that it comes from the Lord. Therefore, God doesn't need *our* help, because He's the one helping us! So, stop trying to play God, and remember we need to "look to the hills from whence cometh our help." Be Blessed!

Psalm 121:1-2

DAILY REFLECTIONS

JANUARY 15

God's Assurance

Whatever we may have need of, God is "Just a Prayer Away" and will attend to our cry. So, when we find ourselves in a tight spot, we can't waste our time worrying and fretting over it. We must take it to God and let Him fix it. Therefore, "Do not be anxious about anything, but in everything, by prayer and petition, with thankfulness, present your requests to God." Be Blessed!

Philippians 4:6

DAILY REFLECTIONS

JANUARY 16

Life's Seasons

There have been quite a few tropical storms and hurricanes over the years, and they seem to be getting worse and worse. It definitely makes us think about what's important in life. We're in a time where we can no longer take life for granted. "There is a time for everything, and a season for every activity under heaven." So, we should live our lives in faith; striving to be all that we can be for the time that we are privileged to be here. Be Blessed!

Ecclesiastes 3:1

DAILY REFLECTIONS

_____
_____
_____
_____
_____
_____
_____
_____
_____
_____

JANUARY 17

Protection

Psalm 46:1 says, "God is our refuge and our strength; a very present help in the time of trouble." Therefore, whenever we are going through difficult times, we must remember God is with us in the struggle. Because He is with us, He can speak "peace" to our storms, deliverance for our souls, and "unspeakable joy" to our hearts! So, no matter what we're going through, or how difficult it may seem, remember that God sees our struggle and help is on the way! Be Blessed!

Psalm 46:1, 1 Peter 1:8

DAILY REFLECTIONS

JANUARY 18

Faith

Now is definitely a time when we need faith. So much is happening all around us, there is no way we can make it if we don't walk in faith. If we look at things through our natural eyes, we will get discouraged. But if we focus our attention on God, we can still have hope. "Find rest, O my soul, in God alone; my hope comes from Him. He alone is my rock and my salvation; He is my fortress, I will not be shaken. My salvation and my honor depend on God; He is my mighty rock, my refuge. Trust in Him at all times, O people; pour out your hearts to Him, for God is our refuge." Be Blessed!

Psalm 62:5-8

DAILY REFLECTIONS

JANUARY 19

Thankfulness

When things are going your way, it's easy to praise God. The difficulty comes when everything falls apart. It's not easy to be thankful when your bills are due and you don't know how you're going to pay them, or when you've been diagnosed with a serious illness and the doctor isn't giving you much hope, and especially when your heart has been broken and you are in the depths of despair! But those are the times when you need to praise God the most, because that is how you get the victory. You need to let the enemy know (just like Shadrach, Meshach, and Abednego) that even if your lights get cut off, your sickness isn't healed, or your heart is still aching, God is still God, and He is still able! "Shadrach, Meshach and Abednego replied to the king, "O Nebuchadnezzar, we do not need to defend ourselves before you in this matter. If we are thrown into the blazing furnace, the God we serve is able to save us from it, and He will rescue us from your hand, O king. But even if He does not, we want you to know, O king, that we will not serve your gods or worship the image of gold you have set up." Be Blessed!

Daniel 3:16-18

DAILY REFLECTIONS

___
___
___
___
___
___
___
___
___

JANUARY 20

Spiritual Gifts

God has given all of us gifts and talents. We often look at others' gifts and stand in awe of them. But God has gifted all of us with unique, special gifts. The question is, are we using them? "We have different gifts, according to the grace given us. If a man's gift is prophesying, let him use it in proportion to his faith. If it is serving, let him serve; if it is teaching, let him teach; if it is encouraging, let him encourage; if it is contributing to the needs of others, let him give generously; if it is leadership, let him govern diligently; if it is showing mercy, let him do it cheerfully." Whatever God calls us to do, He will equip us to do! Be Blessed!

Romans 12:6-8

DAILY REFLECTIONS

JANUARY 21

Trust

God will move us out of our comfort zone when He's getting ready to do something big in our lives. If it were left up to us, we would never change, grow, or stretch ourselves. But God has destined us for greatness, so we can't settle for just being ordinary. God has purposed us to be extraordinary people! He empowers us to be able to see beyond the right here and the right now. We have to be able to believe in what He can do, and not only in what we see. God is much greater than the box we put Him in, and so are we, as long as we are walking with Him. We can't let the enemy hold us back anymore because of our fear of the unknown. We don't have to be afraid, because God has got our backs. "Where can I go from your Spirit? Where can I flee from your presence? If I go up to the heavens, you are there; if I make my bed in the depths, you are there. If I rise on the wings of the dawn, if I settle on the far side of the sea, even there your hand will guide me, your right hand will hold me fast." "There is nothing too hard for God." We need only to trust in Him! Be Blessed!

Psalm 139:7-10, Jeremiah 32:17

DAILY REFLECTIONS

JANUARY 22

Perseverance

Hebrews 10:35-39 says, "Do not throw away your confidence; it will be richly rewarded. You need to persevere so that when you have done the will of God, you will receive what He has promised. For in just a little while, "He who is coming will come and will not delay. But my righteous one will live by faith. And if he shrinks back, I will not be pleased with him. But we are not of those who shrink back and are destroyed, but of those who believe and are saved." So, because we are His righteous ones, we must persevere and live by faith. Keep on keeping on! Be Blessed!

Hebrews 10:35-39

DAILY REFLECTIONS

_____
_____
_____
_____
_____
_____
_____
_____
_____

JANUARY 23

Forgiveness

Isn't it good to know that even when we fall short, we still have a loving God who is there to forgive us and welcome us back into His flock? God desires for all of us to be saved. Therefore, He is concerned when even one of us goes astray! So, if we recognize that we have done wrong and confess it to Him, He is standing there with open arms ready to cleanse us of all unrighteousness. "If we confess our sins, He is faithful and just and will forgive us our sins and purify us from all unrighteousness." So, we should never feel that we've messed up so badly that we can't be forgiven! God is standing at the door of our souls waiting for us to ask Him to come in! "I stand at the door and knock." So, don't just stand there, open up the door and let Him in! Be Blessed!

1 John 1:9, Revelation 3:20

DAILY REFLECTIONS

JANUARY 24

Faith

I had "bedside Baptist" with a few TV church services this morning. The first service I watched talked about "Nothing to Lose," the second was about "Breakthrough Faith," the next was about "God Having a Plan," and the last was "Going to the Other Side of the Deep." I thought it was interesting that although they had different titles, they coincided with one another. The first one stated that we must take risks in life if we're going to walk in faith; all the other sermons said the same, just with different words. Walking in faith means we won't always know what the outcome is going to be. We must trust in God and move forward believing that God will do just what He said He would do. We don't have to see it first...we only have to believe it! "For we walk by faith and not by sight." Be Blessed!

2 Corinthians 5:7

DAILY REFLECTIONS

JANUARY 25

Encouragement

We've all heard the scripture, "and the truth will set you free." But have you ever thought about how hard it is to face the truth? It can be staring us in the face, but we don't want to see it or acknowledge it. Why it is so hard to see what is right in front of us? It's probably because it's easier to stay in denial then deal with it. When we become willing to face the truth, we'll have to deal with whatever the truth is. Most of us don't want to do that. The problem is that until we confront our situations, nothing will ever change. We'll keep going through the same things over and over again until we learn the lesson and determine to do things differently. God wants to do something new in our lives, but we have to be open and willing to receive it! So, confront your situations in boldness today, and determine to do something different! Be Blessed!

John 8:32

DAILY REFLECTIONS

JANUARY 26

Discipline

Discipline and self-control go hand in hand. You can't have one without the other, but if you don't have either one, you're headed for trouble! "Say no to ungodliness and worldly passions, and to live self-controlled, upright and godly lives in this present age, while we wait for the blessed hope—the glorious appearing of our great God and Savior, Jesus Christ." Be Blessed!

Titus 2:12-13

DAILY REFLECTIONS

JANUARY 27

Encouragement

God never puts more on us than we can bear. Therefore, if we're feeling overburdened, it's because we're trying to do it all by ourselves. Jesus said, "Come to me all who are weary and burdened, and I will give you rest." So, learn how to rest in the arms of the Lord. Do your best, then rest. Be Blessed!

Matthew 11:28

DAILY REFLECTIONS

JANUARY 28

Compassion

I get so much joy when I see how giving and compassionate people are around the holidays. However, we need to have the same spirit of giving and compassion all year round. Jesus stated that the way we treat other people is a reflection on how we will treat Him. "For I was hungry and you gave Me nothing to eat, I was thirsty and you gave Me nothing to drink, I was a stranger and you did not invite Me in, I needed clothes and you did not clothe Me, I was sick and in prison and you did not look after Me… I tell you the truth, whatever you did not do for one of the least of these; you did not do for Me." Think about that! Be Blessed!

Matthew 25:42-45

DAILY REFLECTIONS

JANUARY 29

Rest

So often you struggle and become frustrated with your issues because you are trying to handle them all by yourself. Jesus said, "Come to me, all you who are weary and burdened, and I will give you rest. Take my yoke upon you and learn from me, for I am gentle and humble in heart, and you will find rest for your souls." So, why not take Jesus at His Word and find rest for your soul? Be Blessed!

Matthew 11:28-29

DAILY REFLECTIONS

JANUARY 30

Faith

How much of your day is spent trying to please other people? Unless God is the person you're trying to please, you're doing it all in vain! Since God is the One who created us and put us here for a divine purpose, that is Whom we should aim to please. Hebrews 11:6 tell us "without faith it is impossible to please God." Therefore, we should be doing everything we can to build up our faith! "By faith Abraham, even though he was past age–and Sarah herself was barren–was enabled to become a father because he considered Him faithful who had made the promise." Don't wait until you see the evidence to believe, exercise your faith now! "Now faith is the substance of things hoped for, the evidence of things not seen." Be Blessed!

Hebrews 11

DAILY REFLECTIONS

_____
_____
_____
_____
_____
_____
_____
_____
_____

JANUARY 31

Judgment

How many of us have been the victim of mistaken identity? I don't mean the kind of mistaken identity where someone goes to jail because they look a lot like someone who committed a crime. I'm talking about when someone misjudges our character based on how we look, or by what someone else says about us. Unfortunately, we live in a world where people do that every day. It is a fact in today's society that a person is even judged by their credit report. Insurance companies, prospective employers, banks, lending institutions, etc. now equate our credit score with our character! But just as a credit score is an unfair judge of someone's character, so are some of the judgments we place on people. I am so thankful that I serve a God who does not judge me by my outer appearance or slanderous gossip, but instead chooses to look at my heart. "The Lord does not look at the things man looks at. Man looks at the outward appearance, but the Lord looks at the heart." As children of God, we should follow His example and base our impression of people on what's in their heart! Be Blessed!

1 Samuel 16:7

DAILY REFLECTIONS

FEBRUARY 1

Destiny

Life is too short to waste it being miserable. Find out what your passion in life is, and then do it. You don't want to die with your passion still in you because that would make you "buried treasure." We have all been gifted with something, and when we don't use those gifts, we deprive others of the blessings of experiencing them. So, live your life to the fullest and bless all those you come in contact with! "Whatever you have learned or received or heard from Me, or seen in Me–put it into practice. And the God of peace will be with you." Be Blessed!

Philippians 4:9

DAILY REFLECTIONS

FEBRUARY 2

Faith

There is a saying, "God works in mysterious ways." That may be true, but not all the time. God will often lay everything out in front of us, we just refuse to see it. We know what we're supposed to do, but because of fear, or a lack of confidence, we hesitate in moving forward. It's not because we don't know what to do, we are just afraid to do it! Stepping out in faith is very hard to do, but it is something we desperately need to do. If we waited until we understood or could figure out what God was doing, we would never do anything! God told Abraham to leave his country and go to the land He would show him, and Abraham went. He didn't stand around trying to figure out why God would ask him to leave his people and go to an unknown destination. In fact, he didn't ask any questions at all. *He just went!* And that is exactly what we need to do. Step out in faith and just do it. Be Blessed!

Genesis 12:1-4

DAILY REFLECTIONS

_____
_____
_____
_____
_____
_____
_____
_____
_____
_____

FEBRUARY 3

Encouragement

It is so easy for us to be misled. If we are not strong in our convictions, we can easily be led astray. Satan knows our weaknesses and insecurities, and he makes it his job to torment us with them. But he does not have that kind of power over us. He can only do what we allow him to do. Therefore, don't give him your time, your mind or your attention. You must resist him, and he will flee. It's just like anything else—if you don't give it life, then it can't survive. So, when the enemy comes knocking at your door, don't let him in! "Get behind me, Satan! You are a stumbling block to me; you do not have in mind the things of God, but the things of men." "For it is written: Worship the Lord your God, and serve Him only." Then the devil left him and the angels came and attended Him." "Resist the devil and he will flee." Be Blessed!

Matthew 4:10-11, 16:23, James 4:7

DAILY REFLECTIONS

FEBRUARY 4

Praise

I am often reminded of how much we need God every hour. We often try to do things by ourselves, but we can't make it without God. Let's face it, we can't even breathe without God. God is the breath of our life, the strength of our life, and everything that encompasses all that we are. Therefore, we truly need Him every hour! "And my God will meet all your needs according to the riches of His glory in Christ Jesus." Be Blessed!

Philippians 4:19

DAILY REFLECTIONS

FEBRUARY 5

Friendship

We will only have a "few real friends" in life. The type of friends we can go to (whatever the situation), and not have to worry about being judged are few and far between. I'm so glad the Lord is a "friend who sticks closer than a brother." God has blessed us with a few of those kind of friends while we are here on Earth. Therefore, we should take care of and cherish the friends God has blessed us with; always being careful not to take them for granted, because in order to have friends, we must first prove ourselves to be friendly! Be Blessed!

Proverbs 18:24

DAILY REFLECTIONS

FEBRUARY 6

Faith

Moses sent twelve men out to survey the "promised land," but Joshua and Caleb were the only ones who saw the possibilities and opportunities. The other ten were afraid and had a negative outlook in what they saw. They even spread a bad report among the Israelites about it. That is why it is so important to be careful about whose report you will believe. It's bad enough that we are our own worst enemies when it comes to how we perceive things. But, we can also be influenced by the lack of faith of others, if we're not careful. Sometimes we need to do just what Caleb did. Stop listening to what people say and go on and possess what God has promised you! Be Blessed!

Numbers 13:27-33

DAILY REFLECTIONS

FEBRUARY 7

Purpose

God has a purpose for our lives, and a destiny we're supposed to fulfill. God told Jonah to go to Nineveh because He had a work for him to do there. Jonah, however, decided he wanted to go to Tarshish instead. Jonah tried to exercise his free will by going to Tarshish instead of where God told him to go. However, he encountered a storm that led him into the very depths of a fish's belly. It was very unpleasant there, and he wasn't enjoying the trip. But even though he was disobedient by trying to go to Tarshish, he ended up in Nineveh anyway. Isn't it funny how we think we can tell God what we're going to do? We were created by God, saved by God, and purposed by God. So, whenever we are out of the will of God, we will not have any peace or enjoyment, therefore, we might as well do what God has purposed us to do! If we let God be our guide, we will never go astray. Be Blessed!

The Book of Jonah

DAILY REFLECTIONS

FEBRUARY 8

Trust

Do you know what it feels like to rest in the arms of Jesus? I think we all know how to worry, fret, and feel anxious. But do we know how to relax and trust God to work things out? We get all worked up trying to figure things out, but that is not our job! Our job is to trust God, and then do what He says. If you will make God Lord over your life, then He will become The Lord of Your Life. There is no way we can make it without Him, so why even try? "'I am the Alpha and Omega,' says the Lord God, 'Who is and Who was and Who is to come, the Almighty.'" Submit your will to Him today and make Him Lord over your life! Be Blessed!

Revelation 1:8

DAILY REFLECTIONS

FEBRUARY 9

Encouragement

Here we are on the brink of another Lenten season. This is a time for reflection on our walk with the Lord, a time for renewal of promises not yet fulfilled, and a time for rejuvenation of goals we know we can achieve. We can have a positive outlook for our lives because, "we can do all things through Christ who strengthens us." So, no matter what obstacles you're trying to overcome, know that you already have the victory! Be Blessed!

Philippians 4:13

DAILY REFLECTIONS

FEBRUARY 10

Encouragement

Do you see a partially full glass of water as half empty or half full? Our perception will always determine our outlook on life. Therefore, if you sow seeds of doubt, you will reap a harvest of disappointments. Learn to expand your vision and live a life full of expectancy! "Do not be deceived: God cannot be mocked. A man reaps what he sows. The one who sows to please his sinful nature, from that nature will reap destruction; the one who sows to please the Spirit, from the Spirit will reap eternal life. Let us not become weary in doing good, for at a proper time we will reap a harvest if we do not give up." Be Blessed!

Galatians 6:7-9

DAILY REFLECTIONS

FEBRUARY 11

Change

So often we quote the scripture, "For He is faithful that promised." But can God say the same thing about us? How many times do we promise God to get our lives back on track only to backslide again and again? How many times do we waver back and forth about something we *know* God has told us? God's Word doesn't change, and neither does He! "Jesus Christ is the same yesterday and today and forever." Therefore, it is us who needs to change. We need to change and renew our minds to line up with God's Word. We need to change our thoughts to think about "whatever is true, whatever is noble, whatever is right, whatever is lovely, whatever is admirable—if anything is excellent or praiseworthy—think about such things." We need to change our double-mindedness to an unshaken faith! No matter what the situation or circumstances look like, we will not be moved, because "The righteous shall live by faith." Be Blessed!

Hebrews 13:8, Philippians 4:8, Romans 1:17

DAILY REFLECTIONS

FEBRUARY 12

Vision

Before anything can ever come to pass in your life, you must first see it in your mind. You can exchange those false images that have been flooding your mind with positive images of what you want to become. If you want to lose weight, imagine yourself at the weight you want to be. If you want to start a business, picture yourself on the cover of *Fortune 500* magazine. If you've been running from commitment, envision yourself happily married, etc. You can be whatever you set your mind to be. The key is setting your mind to do it. It may not be easy, but it is possible, for "nothing is impossible with God." Be Blessed!

Matthew 19:26

DAILY REFLECTIONS

FEBRUARY 13

Deliverance

For those who are feeling under attack by the enemy today, read Psalm 3 and be reminded that God is our strength and shield, and He is the lifter of our head! Be Blessed!

Psalm 3

O Lord, how many are my foes! How many rise up against me!

Many are saying of me, "God will not deliver him." Selah

But you are a shield around me, O Lord; you bestow glory on me and lift up my head.

To the Lord I cry aloud, and He answers me from His holy hill. Selah

I lie down and sleep; I wake again, because the Lord sustains me.

I will not fear the tens of thousands drawn up against me on every side.

Arise, O Lord! Deliver me, O my God! Strike all my enemies on the jaw; break the teeth of the wicked.

From the Lord comes deliverance. May your blessing be on your people. Selah

DAILY REFLECTIONS

FEBRUARY 14

Love

Valentine's Day can be very difficult for people who don't have a significant other in their life. The media makes a big frenzy about this, and everyone that can capitalize on it will. Even though Valentine's Day focuses on and caters to those in love, it can also be an opportunity for you to reach out and express love to someone who might not ordinarily receive it. Call someone who does not have a significant other and wish them a Happy Valentine's Day. You may be the only person they hear from today. "Love is patient, love is kind, It does not envy, it does not boast, it is not proud. It is not rude, it is not self-seeking, it is not easily angered, it keeps no record of wrongs. Love does not delight in evil, but rejoices with the truth. It always protects, always trusts, always hopes, always perseveres. Love never fails." Be Blessed!

HAPPY VALENTINE'S DAY!

1 Corinthians 13:4-8

DAILY REFLECTIONS

FEBRUARY 15

Destiny

Stepping out of our comfort zones is not easy. Most of us want to stick with what we know or whatever the status quo is. It takes faith to go beyond what the eye can see. That's exactly what we need to do, though, in order to reach our full potential. Don't settle for mediocre when you can have God's best! "For I know the plans I have for you," declares the Lord, "plans to prosper you and not to harm you, plans to give you hope and a future." Be Blessed!

Jeremiah 29:11

DAILY REFLECTIONS

FEBRUARY 16

Trust

Don't be afraid to go to the next level! God is trying to do something new in your life, but you keep slowing down the process because you're afraid of the unknown. God will never take you to anything He can't see you through. Therefore, you can trust Him to work all things out for your good! "He who began a good work in you will carry it on to completion." Be Blessed!

Romans 8:28, Philippians 1:6

DAILY REFLECTIONS

FEBRUARY 17

Love

When I think of the month of February, I always associate it with love. I guess it's because of Valentine's Day, and the theme of love that goes along with it. It's always a good time to check out your "love walk." We all need a reminder occasionally to help us remember God's greatest commandment. "Love the Lord your God with all your heart and with all your soul and with all your mind. This is the first and greatest commandment." Be Blessed!

Matthew 22:37-38

DAILY REFLECTIONS

FEBRUARY 18

Trust

God is the same—yesterday, today and forever. Always faithful and always true. If He said that He would do it, it will come to pass. There is nothing too big or great for Him to handle. Even when we think it's something He's never seen before, God says, "there is nothing new under the sun." Just put your trust in Him, and He will see you through! Be Blessed!

Ecclesiastes 1:9

DAILY REFLECTIONS

FEBRUARY 19

Encouragement

Some days will be harder to get through than others. But always remember, no matter how hard it gets, God is more than able to see you through. No one ever said life would be easy, or that it would be fair. Just getting up each morning and putting one foot in front of the other may be all that some people can do that day. But if you keep getting up and keep putting one foot in front of the other, eventually, you will get to where you need to go! "As for God, His way is perfect; the word of the Lord is flawless. He is a shield for all who take refuge in Him. For who is God besides the Lord? And who is the Rock except our God? It is God who arms me with strength and makes my way perfect." So, even on those dreary days, hold your head up and be encouraged, because God will truly be "the lifter of our head." Be Blessed!

Psalm 3:3, 18:30-32

DAILY REFLECTIONS

FEBRUARY 20

God's Instructions for Living

I challenge you to read Romans 12 in its entirety. It is truly a map of how we are to live our lives. It tells us that we must present our bodies as a living sacrifice unto God, and then we have to change our way of thinking so we can follow God's good and perfect will for our lives. It goes on to talk about the different gifts that God has given each of us, and how we are to love and live peaceably with one another. If we continue to walk in love, even when others don't treat us right, we will overcome evil with good. Be Blessed!

Romans 12

DAILY REFLECTIONS

FEBRUARY 21

Thankfulness

As children of God, we get to experience God's favor over and over again. But each time I receive it, I still get excited because I know I really don't deserve it. God is such an awesome God that He blesses me anyway! If I had 10,000 tongues, I couldn't thank Him enough! "Because of the Lord's great love we are not consumed, for His compassions never fail." Thank you, Lord, for Your grace and mercy! Be Blessed!

Lamentations 3:22

DAILY REFLECTIONS

FEBRUARY 22

"Crazy" Faith

Sometimes God asks us to exercise "crazy faith." That's the kind of faith that doesn't make any sense. You don't see any way out or any way that things can work out, but God challenges you to step out in faith anyway. Abraham exercised "crazy faith" when he went forth as God instructed him, even though He didn't know where he was going. The same way that God was faithful to Abraham in the end, He will be with us, also, if we don't get weary and give up. So, "let us hold unswervingly to the hope we profess, for He who promised is faithful." Be Blessed!

Galatians 6:9, Hebrews 10:23

DAILY REFLECTIONS

FEBRUARY 23

Worry-Free Faith

We often try to face our obstacles by ourselves. Why do we want that when God is standing right there willing and able to help us? There's no need to worry...no need to fret...God has never failed us yet! "You will not have to fight this battle. Take up your positions; stand firm and see the deliverance the Lord will give you, O Judah and Jerusalem. Do not be afraid; do not be discouraged. Go out to face them tomorrow, and the Lord will be with you." Be Blessed!

2 Chronicles 20:17

DAILY REFLECTIONS

_____
_____
_____
_____
_____
_____
_____
_____
_____

FEBRUARY 24

Under His Hedge of Protection

" Taste and see that the Lord is Good; Blessed is the Man who takes Refuge in Him." What better promise of refuge can you ask for? There's no safer place to be than under the hedge of God's protection. Seek His refuge today and rest in the assurance of His protection. "The Lord is my rock, my fortress and my deliverer; my God is my rock, in whom I take refuge." Be Blessed!

Psalms 18:2, 34:8

DAILY REFLECTIONS

FEBRUARY 25

God Fights Our Battles

Are you still trying to figure out how God is going to work things out in your life? Everything seems a mess, and you can't see how you're going to make it? Well, it's not for you to figure out! "The battle is not yours, it's the Lord's." I know it's hard having blind faith, but that's exactly what you have to have. You keep stressing yourself out trying to do what only God can do. So, just do your best, then rest! "Do not be afraid or discouraged because of this vast army. For the battle is not yours, but God's." Be Blessed!

2 Chronicles 20:15

DAILY REFLECTIONS

FEBRUARY 26

Peace

One of the worst things we can do is to take the peace of God for granted. We continue to live in chaos when God has promised us "perfect peace, if we keep our minds focused on Him." He also told us, "do not be anxious about anything, but in everything, by prayer and petition, with Thankfulness, present your requests to God. And the peace of God, which transcends all understanding, will guard your hearts and minds in Christ Jesus." So, why then, do we continue to be content living out of balance, crazy, chaotic lives, when we can have God's promise of peace? We have to determine today to stop allowing the devil to keep us bound to the dysfunction of our pasts and "press toward the mark for the prize of the high calling of God in Christ Jesus." Be Blessed!

Isaiah 26:3, Philippians 3:14, 4:6-7

DAILY REFLECTIONS

FEBRUARY 27

Gentleness

❝A gentle answer turns away wrath, but a harsh word stirs up anger." So what kind of witness for God do you want to be? One who turns away wrath, or one who stirs up anger? Be Blessed!

Proverbs 15:1

DAILY REFLECTIONS

_____
_____
_____
_____
_____
_____
_____
_____
_____

FEBRUARY 28

Fullness in God

Do you surround yourselves with people who uplift you and encourage you along your life's journey? If not, you should. God has a plan for your life, and those you choose to have in your circle should be on the same path you are. When you go through difficult times in your life, can you count on those around you to be there to catch you when you fall? Well, I hope they can, but even if they can't, God certainly will! "May the God of hope fill you with all joy and peace as you trust in Him, so that you may overflow with hope by the power of the Holy Spirit." Be Blessed!

Romans 15:13

DAILY REFLECTIONS

FEBRUARY 29

Forgiveness

Forgiveness is a powerful thing. When you have resentment towards someone, you not only hurt them, but you keep yourself in bondage, as well. There is nothing more draining to your spirit than holding onto old hurts and resentments. You must learn to forgive people that have hurt you, so you will be forgiven as well. "And when you stand praying, if you hold anything against anyone, forgive him, so that your Father in Heaven may forgive you." Be Blessed!

Mark 11:25

DAILY REFLECTIONS

MARCH 1

God's Promises

In our darkest hours, it is so easy to get frustrated and quit. But, if you are walking in faith, quitting is not an option! Times may get hard and situations may seem bleak, but we must always remember that God is still in control. If He said that He would do it, it will come to pass. "Commit thy way unto the Lord; trust also in Him, and He shall bring it to pass." God has not forgotten His promise to you! "Lo, I am with you always, even unto the end of the world." Be Blessed!

Psalm 37:5, Matthew 28:20

DAILY REFLECTIONS

MARCH 2

Prayer

When you pray, do you expect to hear from God? Do you take time to listen to hear His voice? God desires to fellowship with you, and one of the ways to do that is through prayer. But effective communication involves talking *and* listening. So, the next time you pray, expect God to answer and then listen to what He has to say! "In the morning, O LORD, you hear my voice; in the morning, I lay my requests before you and wait in expectation." Be Blessed!

Psalm 5:3

DAILY REFLECTIONS

MARCH 3

God's Example

When people see you in action, are you a shining example of God's evidence in your life? Matthew 5:3-11 describes "The Beatitudes," followed by a charge to you to be a witness for God's Glory. "You are the salt of the earth. But if the salt loses its saltiness, how can it be made salty again? It is no longer good for anything, except to be thrown out and trampled by men." "You are the light of the world. A city on a hill cannot be hidden. Neither do people light a lamp and put it under a bowl. Instead, they put it on its stand, and it gives light to everyone in the house. In the same way, let your light shine before men, that they may see your good deeds and praise your Father in Heaven." So, remember to let your light so shine before men that they will see your life and want to know "what must I do to be saved?" Be Blessed!

Matthew 5:3-16, Acts 16:30

DAILY REFLECTIONS

MARCH 4

Redemption

All of us have the potential to be manipulative and controlling. It doesn't matter how nice, spiritual, or mature we are—once we learn that if we do certain things we can get people to do what we want them to do, it's on! If we learn that pouting, yelling, withdrawing our love, or giving the silent treatment, works to our advantage, we begin doing it without even knowing it. However, we know that this kind of behavior is not from God. Therefore, we must ask God to come into our hearts and change those things that are not like Him. God will do His part; the question is, can we? "Let us draw near to God with a sincere heart in full assurance of faith, having our hearts sprinkled to cleanse us from a guilty conscience and having our bodies washed with pure water." Be Blessed!

Hebrews 10:22

DAILY REFLECTIONS

_____
_____
_____
_____
_____
_____
_____
_____
_____

MARCH 5

Protection

In times of trouble when you are tempted to wonder if God has forgotten you, meditate on Psalm 37:23-28. It says, "If the Lord delights in a man's way, He makes his steps firm; though he stumble, he will not fall, for the Lord upholds him with His hand. I was young and now I am old, yet I have never seen the righteous forsaken or their children begging bread. They are always generous and lend freely; their children will be blessed. Turn from evil and do good; then you will dwell in the land forever. For the Lord loves the just and will not forsake His faithful ones. They will be protected forever." Be Blessed!

Psalm 37:23-28

DAILY REFLECTIONS

_____
_____
_____
_____
_____
_____
_____
_____
_____

MARCH 6

Negativity (Renewing Your Mind)

Are you a negative thinking person? Do you tend to look at situations in a pessimistic way? If you answered yes to either of these questions, please be advised that God wants to renew your mind! God did not send His Son to die for you so that you would live a negative, unhappy, unfulfilled life. "But the Son of Man came to seek and to save what was lost." Therefore, since you know you have the gift of eternal life through Jesus Christ, you should not have a negative outlook about anything. Instead, you should renew your mind to be more like the mind of Christ. "Finally, brethren, whatsoever things are true, whatsoever things are honest, whatsoever things are just, whatsoever things are pure, whatsoever things are lovely, whatsoever things are of good report; if there be any virtue, and if there be any praise, think on these things." If you think about these things, it will be impossible for you to think negatively! Be Blessed!

Matthew 18:11, Philippians 4:8

DAILY REFLECTIONS

MARCH 7

God's Plan for Your Life

If you call someone, don't you expect them to answer? Why then, do we ignore God when He calls us? He promises to listen when we call Him, so why aren't we doing the same for Him? You might as well answer Him, because He will never allow you to have any peace as long as you are outside of His will. There is no need to fear what God has in store for you. We may not be able to see what lies ahead, but God does, and He promises to work it all out for our good! "For I know the plans I have for you," declares the Lord, "plans to prosper you and not to harm you, plans to give you hope and a future. Then you will call upon me and come and pray to me, and I will listen to you. You will seek me and find me when you seek me with all your heart." Be Blessed!

Jeremiah 29:11-13

DAILY REFLECTIONS

MARCH 8

Hope

If we are hoping for God to do something in our lives, we must wait in tiptoe expectation! We should start to get excited because we *expect* God to move on our behalf! If you have hope that means you will start preparing for your blessing because you honestly believe you are going to receive it. I would much rather live a life full of hope, than one filled with doubt and despair! "We wait in hope for the Lord; He is our Help and our Shield. In Him our hearts rejoice, for we trust in His holy name. May your unfailing love rest upon us, O LORD, even as we put our hope in you." Be Blessed!

Psalm 33:20-22

DAILY REFLECTIONS

MARCH 9

Positive Speaking

Since "death and life are in the power of the tongue," let's make a conscious effort to speak positive things with our mouths. We also need to combat the enemy's lies with positive affirmations and tear down the strongholds he is building around us. For example, if we're struggling with depression, we should thank God in advance for giving us "unspeakable joy." Or if we know that we can continue to be double-minded in our prayer life and faith walk, thank God for giving us a faith that does not waver. Or if we are feeling lost and all alone, thank God for "never leaving us or forsaking us," etc. The lists go on and on ... But remember, we need to replace all of Satan's lies with God's truths. We must meditate on God's word so we will be able to speak it in our time of need! "Thy word is a lamp unto my feet, and a light unto my path." Be Blessed!

Proverbs 18:21, 1 Peter 1:8, Hebrews 13:5, Psalm 119:105

DAILY REFLECTIONS

MARCH 10

Prayer

Heavenly Father,

We come to you as humbly as we know how, asking for your grace and mercy. Lord, we don't always do like we should, but we are eternally grateful to you for loving us despite our sinful ways. We ask you now to forgive us for our sins, those we knowingly commit, and those we commit innocently. We ask you to strengthen us where we are weak and speak peace to our restless souls. Lord, we can't make it without you, so we are standing on your promise that "you will never leave us nor forsake us." Please heal us, deliver us, and keep us under your hedge of protection which keeps us from all hurt, harm, and danger. Lord, we need you in a mighty way! We are hard-pressed on every side, but we know that "nothing is impossible or too difficult for you." So, even though some may be in need of healing (physical or emotional), deliverance (habits, strongholds, or past hurts or pains), or financial prosperity (bills paid, steady employment, promotion, etc.), "you are more than able to do exceedingly above anything we can ask, think, or imagine." So, we stand in tiptoe expectation awaiting the glorious manifestation of our prayers, knowing that "He that began this good work in us is able to complete it." Lord, we love you and adore you, and we will never place anyone or anything before you! Amen.

Deuteronomy 31:8, Ephesians 3:20, Philippians 1:6

DAILY REFLECTIONS

MARCH 11

Spiritual Maturity

Isn't it funny how God matures us? He puts us in situations that make us look back over our past and see how He has worked miracles in our lives! Why then, do we worry about our future? If He made a way before, He can do it again! We can walk in confidence because of the history we have with God. He did not bring us this far to leave us now. Therefore, we can rejoice in knowing that "our steps are ordered by the Lord." When in doubt, read the 23rd Psalm:

> The Lord is my shepherd; I shall not want.
> He maketh me to lie down in green pastures; He leadeth me beside the still waters.
> He restoreth my soul; He leadeth me in the paths of righteousness for His name's sake.
> Yea, though I walk through the valley of the shadow of death, I will fear no evil: for thou art with me; thy rod and thy staff they comfort me.
> Thou preparest a table before me in the presence of mine enemies; though anointest my head with oil; my cup runneth over.
> Surely goodness and mercy shall follow me all the days of my life, and I will dwell in the house of the Lord forever.
>
> Psalm 23, 37:23

DAILY REFLECTIONS

MARCH 12

Judgment

Most of us have heard the expression, "What's done in the dark will come to light." We often do things we know aren't right, and then try to justify our actions. But God knows what's really in our heart and He knows our true motive. If our intentions are not honorable, God will judge us and give us our just reward. The Bible says, "we reap what we sow." So, if we sow lies and deception that is what we will reap. "My conscience is clear, but that does not make me innocent. It is the Lord who judges me. Therefore, judge nothing before the appointed time; wait till the Lord comes. He will bring to light what is hidden in darkness and will expose the motives of men's hearts." Be Blessed!

Galatians 6:7, 1 Corinthians 4:4-5

DAILY REFLECTIONS

MARCH 13

Defeating the Enemy

Things may seem to be going crazy in your life right now, and you feel as if you're under attack. Well, the truth is, you probably are! Don't get discouraged, though, because the enemy is only attacking you because you are tearing his kingdom down. He doesn't bother people that are already following him, only those that are a threat to him. But if you keep your mind focused on God and remember what He said in His word, you can defeat the devil! Make no mistake about it, the enemy wants to destroy you *and* your family. "Your enemy the devil prowls around like a roaring lion looking for someone to devour. Resist him, standing firm in the faith, because you know your brothers throughout the world are undergoing the same kinds of sufferings." When you continue to stand on God's promises and hold onto your faith, you can rest assured that God will always vindicate you! Be Blessed!

1 Peter 5:8-9

DAILY REFLECTIONS

MARCH 14

Waiting on God

Have you ever prayed for something for so long that you got tired of waiting? Well, join the club! I think we've all been in that boat at one time or another. The secret to waiting, though, is believing that God will eventually show up. Our job is to trust His timing, and His will for our lives. "Your righteousness reaches to the skies, O God, you have done great things. Who, O God, is like you? Though you have made me see troubles, many and bitter, you will restore my life again; from the depths of the earth you will again bring me up. You will increase my honor and comfort me once again." Thank you, Lord for your mighty works! You alone are worthy of our praise! Be Blessed!

Psalm 71:19-21

DAILY REFLECTIONS

MARCH 15

Stand Firm

Life will throw you some curves, but you must learn to roll with the punches. When you've done everything you know to do, just keep standing firm. Don't give up! Keep on praying. Keep on believing. Keep holding onto your faith. God is not through blessing you! "Therefore put on the full armor of God, so that when the day of evil comes, you may be able to stand your ground, and after you have done everything, to stand." Be Blessed!

Ephesians 6:13

DAILY REFLECTIONS

MARCH 16

Negative Thinking

We must always keep our minds focused on the positive things in life. Even if we grew up around negative circumstances, we have to make up our minds to change our way of thinking. You will always get whatever you expect. So, if you go around saying, "things never work out for me," or "I can't do anything right," or "I always get the short end of the stick," etc., then that's exactly what you will get! It will become a self-fulfilling prophecy. Think about the Peanuts' character, Charlie Brown, and how bad he always professed his life to be. He was a good guy, but he always spoke negatively about his circumstances. He would always walk around with a sad story to tell and that is exactly what his life became! SAD! So, determine not to live your life in negativity. Instead, think on "whatever is true, whatever is noble, whatever is right, whatever is pure, whatever is lovely, whatever is admirable—if anything is excellent or praiseworthy—think about such things." You will become whatever you think you are! Be Blessed!

Philippians 4:8

DAILY REFLECTIONS

MARCH 17

Patience

We've all heard the expression, "good things come to those who wait." But the waiting is *so hard,* isn't it? God's timing is definitely not the same as ours, and I'll be the first to say that sometimes I wish He would work a little faster! But God knows all, and is in all, so we must learn to trust His timing and His ways. "And the God of all grace, who called you to His eternal glory in Christ, after you have suffered a little while, will Himself restore you and make you strong, firm and steadfast." Be Blessed!

1 Peter 5:10

DAILY REFLECTIONS

MARCH 18

Hearing God's Voice

Hearing the voice of God is not easy because you often confuse God's voice with your own selfish desires. If the actions don't line up with what God says in His word, then it's not His voice you're hearing. "God is not a man that He should lie," so if it is His good and perfect will for your life, it will line-up with His word. "Then you will be able to test and approve what God's will is—His good, pleasing and perfect will." So, "Dear friends, do not believe every spirit, but test the spirits to see whether they are from God." Be Blessed!

Numbers 23:19, Romans 12:2, 1 John 4:1

DAILY REFLECTIONS

MARCH 19

Confession

Do you consider yourself to be an honest person? Are you honest with other people? Are you honest with yourself? Most importantly, are you honest with God? If you can't answer yes to all of those questions, ask God to give you the boldness and courage to face whatever it is that you're afraid to be honest about. God already knows the truth and so does everyone else, so you might as well go on and admit it to yourself! The childhood story about the emperor with no clothes is a good example. Everybody could see that he didn't have on any clothes except him! There is no shame in admitting you have faults. Everyone has them! But until you recognize and admit that you have them, you can't do anything about them. God wants to do a "new thing" in you; however, He needs a broken and contrite spirit before He can move in your situation. Read Psalm 51 in its entirety and see the awesome things God can do in your life if you let Him! Be Blessed!

Psalm 51

DAILY REFLECTIONS

MARCH 20

Faith

Sometimes when we pray, we wonder if we will ever get what we are praying for. "Come and listen, all you who fear God; let me tell you what He has done for me. I cried out to Him with my mouth; His praise was on my tongue. If I had cherished sin in my heart, the Lord would not have listened; but God has surely listened and heard my voice in prayer. Praise be to God, who has not rejected my prayer or withheld His love from me." I can certainly say that God answers prayers when I look back over my life! "For He is faithful that promised." Be Blessed!

Psalm 66:16-20, Hebrews 10:23

DAILY REFLECTIONS

MARCH 21

God's Transforming Power

God can change our nature even when we can't! We try over and over again to change the things we don't like about ourselves, yet still find it to be a struggle. But when we submit our will to God's, He will give us the "peace that surpasses all understanding." So, why struggle when you can rest in the arms of the Lord? "Submit yourselves, then to God" and allow Him to change you into the person He desires you to be! "Therefore, if any man be in Christ, he is a new creation; the old is gone, the new has come." Be Blessed!

Philippians 4:7, James 4:7, 2 Corinthians 5:17

DAILY REFLECTIONS

MARCH 22

Patience

Since we all know the saying, "good things come to those who wait," why do we have such a hard time waiting? I don't know anyone who likes to wait, and I have an extremely hard time doing it myself! But, we must remember that God is looking to see how we will handle ourselves during the waiting period. Will we throw a tantrum and get mad at God, or be jealous of everyone around us that is receiving blessings? "God is no respecter of persons," so if He blesses those around you, He will bless you, too! We just have to wait for God's timing. "For the revelation awaits an appointed time; it speaks of the end and will not prove false. Though it linger, wait for it; it will certainly come and will not delay." God wants to prosper you, so be patient and wait for it! Be Blessed!

Acts 10:34, Habakkuk 2:3

DAILY REFLECTIONS

MARCH 23

Praise

Our God is an awesome God! How often do we take the time to acknowledge that? God has done so much for us, our praise should be non-stop! "I will bless the Lord at all times: His praise shall continually be in my mouth." "Rejoice in the Lord Always and again I say Rejoice." Be Blessed!

Psalm 34:1, Philippians 4:4

DAILY REFLECTIONS

MARCH 24

God's Goodness

" O taste and see that the Lord is good: blessed is the man that trusteth in Him." Start your day reflecting on how good God has been to you. If you do that, you can't help but to be in a good mood! Be Blessed!

Psalm 34:8

DAILY REFLECTIONS

MARCH 25

God Is Our Helper

Who do you go to when you have a problem? A friend? A parent? A spiritual advisor? While these may be the most common options to choose, a much better choice would be to go to God! He is omniscient, omnipresent, omnipotent, and "able to do immeasurably more than you could ever ask or imagine." So, why even think about going anywhere else? "God is our refuge and strength, an ever-present help in trouble." Be Blessed!

Ephesians 3:20, Psalm 46:1

DAILY REFLECTIONS

MARCH 26

Trusting God's Plan

Resting in God should be so easy to do. Yet, we make things hard for ourselves. We keep things bottled up inside, trying to handle everything on our own. God promised "never to leave us nor forsake us," but yet we still doubt. God has proven Himself over and over again; just as He did with the Israelites when He delivered them out of Egypt. But they continued to whine and complain every time things got hard. As a result, what should have been an eleven-day journey took them 40 years! Let's not make the same mistake they did and wander around the same mountain for 40 years. Let's do it the right way and take the shortest route: God's way! "For I know the plans I have for you," declares the Lord, "plans to prosper you and not to harm you, plans to give you hope and a future." He's already paved the way, now it's up to us to walk in it! Be Blessed!

Jeremiah 29:11

DAILY REFLECTIONS

MARCH 27

Seasons of Change

It has been said that the only thing that is constant in life is "change." So, no matter how hard people try to keep things the same, they might as well accept the fact that things are going to change. The economy changes, the cost of living changes, the stock market changes, everything changes! The best thing we can do is learn to adjust to it. "There is a time for everything, and a season for every activity under heaven." So instead of dreading it or getting anxious about it, learn to accept it and keep on going! Be Blessed!

Ecclesiastes 3:1

DAILY REFLECTIONS

MARCH 28

God's Omnipresence

Isn't it wonderful to know that even in the midst of our circumstances, God is right there with us? Jesus said, "Lo, I am with you always, even unto the end of the earth." What an awesome promise that is! When we're going through our storms, He will be right there to see us through! Thank You, God for Jesus! Be Blessed!

Matthew 28:20

DAILY REFLECTIONS

MARCH 29

Obedience

Just as Jesus met Mary Magdalene and the other Mary as they went to tell the disciples that He had risen from the dead, He will meet us too. We often wonder why nothing seems to be happening in our situations. Sometimes God is working things out, although, sometimes He's waiting for us to do our part! God has given us many promises in His Word, however, some of them are conditional. So, before you get angry and frustrated with God, check yourself first! You may be the one holding up the process! "All these blessings will come upon you and accompany you if you obey the Lord your God." Be Blessed!

Matthew 28, Deuteronomy 28:2

DAILY REFLECTIONS

MARCH 30

Generosity

One of the greatest gifts we can ever receive from God is the gift of generosity. It is a wonderful feeling when God blesses us, but it's even more precious when we can pass that blessing on to someone else. It doesn't bring God any glory when we keep our testimonies and our blessings to ourselves. But think of all the lives we can touch when we spread the Word of God through our generosity! God has blessed us in so many ways, why don't you take a moment to be a blessing to someone else today? "Give and it will be given to you. A good measure, pressed down, shaken together and running over, will be poured into your lap. For with the measure you use, it will be measured to you." Be Blessed!

Luke 6:38

DAILY REFLECTIONS

MARCH 31

God's Saving Grace

We should always remember what a sacrifice God made for us by sending His Son to die for us. He not only sent His only Son to die for us, but he also raised Him from the dead to save us and give us the gift of eternal life. We should be eternally grateful for that! "For God so loved the world that He gave His one and only Son, that whoever believes in Him shall not perish but have eternal life. For God did not send His Son into the world to condemn the world, but to save the world through Him." There is no greater love than that! Be Blessed!

John 3:16-17

DAILY REFLECTIONS

___
___
___
___
___
___
___
___

APRIL 1

Humility

The Bible tells us, "Humble yourselves, therefore, under God's might hand, that He may lift you up in due time. "Cast all your anxiety on Him because He cares for you." Therefore, you have to let go of your pride and humble yourself, so He can lift you up! To be humble means to be modest, meek and lowly. In order for God to lift you up, you must first be low. So, if you have an arrogant spirit with a lot of pride, you are not even in a position for God to lift you up. You already "think more highly of yourself than you ought to." Remember, God's promise of lifting you up is tied to you first becoming humble! Be Blessed!

1 Peter 5:6-7, Romans 12:3

DAILY REFLECTIONS

APRIL 2

Insecurity

Insecurity plays a big role in mistrusting people. Insecure people are hesitant to help other people reach their goals in life because they are afraid of following their own dreams. However, if you believe in the principle of reciprocity, you know when you bless others; you will be blessed in return. Therefore, there is no need to be jealous or insecure of others because the same God that blessed them will bless you too! "Be merciful, just as your Father is merciful. "Do not judge, and you will not be judged. Do not condemn, and you will not be condemned. Forgive, and you will be forgiven. Give, and it will be given to you. A good measure, pressed down, shaken together and running over, will be poured into your lap. F or with the measure you use, it will be measured to you." Be Blessed!

Luke 6:36-38

DAILY REFLECTIONS

APRIL 3

Gratefulness

People often take simple pleasures of life for granted. However, if you've ever experienced a loss of any kind, it will make you realize how blessed you really are! "Praise the Lord, O my soul; all my inmost being, praise His holy name. Praise the Lord, O my soul, and forget not all His benefits—who forgives all your sins and heals all your diseases, who redeems your life from the pit and crowns you with love and compassion, who satisfies your desires with good things so that your youth is renewed like the eagle's. The Lord works righteousness and justice for all the oppressed." So, instead of complaining, try praising Him because it is truly a blessing being His child! Be Blessed!

Psalm 103:1-6

DAILY REFLECTIONS

APRIL 4

God's Deliverance

"O magnify the Lord with me, and let us exalt His name together. I sought the Lord, and He heard me, and delivered me from all my fears." Things happen to us in our lives that make us fearful and afraid. But God has assured us that He will answer our cries and deliver us out of all our troubles. The thing we must remember is that <u>God</u> delivers, not <u>us</u>! We can't save ourselves, and we certainly can't save anyone else! So, for those struggling with what to do about their loved ones, who aren't saved or delivered, rest assured that God alone can save them, deliver them, and provide for them. When we try to do things ourselves, what we're saying is that we don't trust God to take care of it, so we need to get involved and help Him out. Do yourself a favor; *let go* and *let God*! "This poor man called, and the Lord heard him; He saved him out of all his troubles. The angel of the Lord encamps around those who fear Him, and He delivers them. O Taste and see that the Lord is good. Blessed is the man who trusteth in Him." Be Blessed!

Psalm 34:4-8

DAILY REFLECTIONS

APRIL 5

Faith

How often do we say we have faith, but our lives aren't bearing any fruit? "Faith without works is dead." If we are truly walking in faith, then we ought to show some signs of it! We can't say we have faith and continually speak words of doubt. Nor can we say we have faith but stay stuck in a rut because we're afraid to move forward to the next level that God is trying to take us to. Stepping out in faith is not easy, but it is very necessary if we are ever going to get where God is trying to lead us. God has promised us a "land flowing with milk and honey," so why are we settling for less? "They gave Moses this account: "We went into the land to which you sent us, and it does flow with milk and honey! Here is its fruit...Then Caleb silenced the people before Moses and said, let us go and take possession of the land, for we can certainly do it." It's time for us to possess the land! Be Blessed!

James 2:17, Numbers 13:27-30

DAILY REFLECTIONS

APRIL 6

Compassion

My great nephew always wants to say a prayer after we say grace over our meal. The amazing thing is, he doesn't say a memorized grace or prayer, he says whatever is on his mind and in his heart (we truly believe he is going to be a preacher when he grows up)! One of the things he said when he prayed this past Easter was, "God help us to be kind to one another." God tells us in His Word, "Be kind and compassionate to one another, forgiving each other, just as in Christ God forgave you." My great nephew may only be 7 years old, but he is already speaking and living God's Word with boldness. How many of us can say we're doing that? Start by following God's instructions and be kind to someone today! Be Blessed!

Ephesians 4:32

DAILY REFLECTIONS

APRIL 7

Encouragement

A few days a week I try to walk for an hour on my treadmill. Every day I want to quit before the hour is up. But after pushing through the pain, I always manage to finish the course. Strangely enough, life is like that, too. We always want to quit when things get hard or become painful, but we need to line ourselves up with people that will encourage us to press on and finish the course! You'll never get anywhere if you hang out with people who don't want to go anywhere either. You must latch onto the coattails of someone who is trying to get to where you want to go. So, when life gets hard, don't give up, just keep pressing on. "For at the proper time we will reap a harvest if we do not give up." Be Blessed!

Galatians 6:9

DAILY REFLECTIONS
___
___
___
___
___
___
___
___
___

APRIL 8

Assurance

" This is the day that the Lord has made, Let us rejoice and be glad in it." No matter how bad your situation may seem today, there is someone worse off than you. If you can remember that when you're having your bad moments, it will help you count your blessings, instead of complaining about what you don't have. Yes, life is hard, and we can't always seem to figure things out. But rest assured, God is still in control and He knows exactly what to do. So, don't waste your time worrying about it anymore, keep your mind focused on the problem-solver, and not on the problem! Be Blessed!

Psalm 118:24

DAILY REFLECTIONS

APRIL 9

Protection

There are several songs that talk about the goodness of being "kept by God." What a wonderful assurance you have as a child of God, to know you have His hedge of protection around you at all times. You don't have to worry about something happening to you when God is not watching, because He never stops watching over you! "He who watches over you will not slumber; indeed, He who watches over Israel will neither slumber nor sleep. The Lord watches over you—the Lord is your shade at your right hand; the sun will not harm you by day, nor the moon by night. The Lord will keep you from all harm—He will watch over your life; the Lord will watch over your coming and going both now and forevermore." Thank God for the promise of being kept by the Lord! He's a Keeper! Be Blessed!

Psalm 121:3-8

DAILY REFLECTIONS

APRIL 10

Salvation

One of the things I've always found interesting about bowling is that you get more than one chance to knock the pins down. If you knock them all down in one try, that's a "strike." However, if you don't knock them all down the first time but knock the rest of them down on your second chance, that's called a "spare." How awesome it is that God did not "spare" His only Son but instead sacrificed Him so that we could have another chance? "Christ was sacrificed once to take away the sins of many people; and He will appear a second time, not to bear sin, but to bring salvation to those who are waiting for Him." Thank God for the second chance He gave us through Jesus Christ! Be Blessed!

Hebrews 9:28

DAILY REFLECTIONS

APRIL 11

Trust

" If God is for us, who can be against us?" We get upset and stressed out because of the things we come up against in life. But, if God is on our side, we don't have to get upset. We have His assurance that "in all things God works for the good of those who love Him, who have been called according to His purpose." Whatever happens to us, God is in the midst working things out for our good. Relax; God has it all under control! Be Blessed!

Romans 8:28-31

DAILY REFLECTIONS

___
___
___
___
___
___
___
___
___

APRIL 12

God's Will for Your Life

Paul told the Thessalonians "Make sure that nobody pays back wrong for wrong, but always try to be kind to each other and to everyone else. Be joyful always; pray continually; give thanks in all circumstances, for this is God's will for you in Christ Jesus." It was good advice then, and it still is today. All we need to do is go and do likewise! Be Blessed!

1 Thessalonians 5:15-18

DAILY REFLECTIONS

APRIL 13

God's Way is the Only Way

Just when you think you're at the end of your rope—God steps in right on time! Many times we pray and nothing seems to happen. But, when we least expect it, things begin to change and turn around. We have to stop putting God in a box! "His ways are not our ways, and His thoughts are not our thoughts." We need to stop trying to figure out how God is going to work things out. All we need to know is that we can trust Him to do it! "Trust in the Lord with all thine heart; and lean not unto thine own understanding. In all thy ways acknowledge Him, and He shall direct thy paths." Be Blessed!

Isaiah 55:8, Proverbs 3:5-6

DAILY REFLECTIONS

APRIL 14

Positive Speaking Leads to Positive Thinking

We must be careful about the things we say. Without even knowing it, we can go against everything we're praying to God for. How many times do you hear yourself say things like, "Good things never happen to me," or "Bad luck seems to follow me." Statements like these cancel out the blessings God is trying to give you! So, get rid of that gloomy attitude and start speaking positive things over your life! Remember, "Death and life are in the power of the tongue." Therefore, you must speak *life*! Be Blessed!

Proverbs 18:21

DAILY REFLECTIONS

APRIL 15

Procrastination

April 15 is the dreaded IRS Tax Day. It is usually the same time every year, but some people procrastinate and wait until the last minute every year. It's understandable if you have to pay, but some people file late for no apparent reason. These same people procrastinate in all aspects of their life. That is a dangerous thing to do. Tomorrow is not promised to any, so we should not put off for tomorrow what we can do today. Tomorrow may never come! Therefore, don't procrastinate any longer. God accepts you just as you are. In fact, it is better to come to Him in a humble and low spirit so that He can lift you up! "Humble yourselves before the Lord and He will lift you up." Be Blessed!

James 4:10

DAILY REFLECTIONS

_____
_____
_____
_____
_____
_____
_____
_____
_____

APRIL 16

Following God's Plan

When children are toddlers they reach a stage where they want to do everything by themselves. They want to feed themselves, dress themselves, and comb their own hair. They want to do it by themselves because they are claiming their independence. They go through this independent stage again once they become teenagers. As a Christian, you may attempt to exercise this same kind of independence with God. You try to do everything on your own and then get frustrated when things don't work out as planned. However, if you remember that God has already made plans for your life and determine to line your plans up with His, then your plans will never fail. "Commit to the Lord whatever you do, and your plans will succeed." Be Blessed!

Proverbs 16:3

DAILY REFLECTIONS

APRIL 17

Be Yourself

Society often tries to pigeonhole people into being who they want them to be. However, we must be true to who God created us to be. Whenever we attempt to be someone we're not, we are out of the will of God. Therefore, it is in our best interest to follow the path that has been set before us. "In Him we have redemption through His blood, the forgiveness of sins, in accordance with the riches of God's grace that He lavished on us with all wisdom and understanding. And He made known to us the mystery of His will according to His good pleasure, which He purposed in Christ, to be put into effect when the times will have reached their fulfillment—to bring all things in heaven and on earth together under one head, even Christ. In Him we were also chosen, having been predestined according to the plan of Him who works out everything in conformity with the purpose of His will, in order that we, who were the first to hope in Christ, might be for the praise of His glory." Be Blessed!

Ephesians 1:7-12

DAILY REFLECTIONS

APRIL 18

Integrity

Have you ever known someone who did a lot of talking, but never really said or did anything worthwhile? Shakespeare wrote in the play *Macbeth*: "a tale told by an idiot, full of sound and fury, signifying nothing." Even back then people knew how to blow a lot of smoke! However, our walk *and* our talk should mean something. If we don't walk in God's love, Paul states in 1 Corinthians that we are nothing. "If I speak in the tongues of men and of angels, but have not love, I am only a resounding gong or a clanging cymbal. If I have the gift of prophecy and can fathom all mysteries and all knowledge, and if I have a faith that can move mountains, but have not love, I am nothing. If I give all I possess to the poor and surrender my body to the flames, but have not love, I gain nothing." So, we should spend less time talking and spend more time walking in love! Be Blessed!

1 Corinthians 13:1-3

DAILY REFLECTIONS

APRIL 19

Dream Chaser

We all have dreams and visions in life, the question is, what are we doing with them? We can sit back and watch everyone else obtain theirs dreams, or we can join them and actively seek after and achieve our own. Whatever God has gifted us to do; He will equip us to do. "A man's gift maketh room for him." So, don't waste any more time, go on and "stir up the gift." Be Blessed!

Proverb 18:16, 2 Timothy 1:6

DAILY REFLECTIONS

APRIL 20

Assurance

It's been said that "it's a woman's prerogative to change her mind." I think that quote was created because of how often women are known to change their minds! But thankfully, God is not like that. We can depend on Him to keep His Word and to fulfill His promises. He doesn't promise something and then take it back. God doesn't change His mind. He stays true to His Word. "I, the Lord, do not change." So, let's take a minute to thank God for that assurance. Be Blessed!

Malachi 3:6

DAILY REFLECTIONS

APRIL 21

God's Sovereignty

God's blessings don't always come the way we think, and He doesn't always do things the way we want Him to. He is a Sovereign God, and He does what He wants...when He wants...and how He wants. Our job is to trust Him and give Him the honor that He is due. We don't have to try to figure out what He is doing, all we need to know is that He *is* doing something! So, Let Go and Let God! Be Blessed!

Isaiah 55:8

DAILY REFLECTIONS

_____
_____
_____
_____
_____
_____
_____
_____

APRIL 22

Forgiveness

There may be times in your life when God seems far away. As much as I can relate to and understand this feeling, we must realize it isn't God that has left us. Usually it is because we have moved away from Him. We get busy in our everyday lives and don't spend that quality time with Him. Or we fall into sin and feel ashamed that we've disappointed God once again. But whatever the reason, just know that God has not forsaken you. "If we confess our sins, He is faithful and just and will forgive us our sins and purify us from all unrighteousness." So, don't move away from God even when you fall short; He is standing by with open arms waiting to forgive and love you unconditionally! Be Blessed!

1 John 1:9

DAILY REFLECTIONS

APRIL 23

Hymns of Praise

Many writers of spiritual songs and hymns wrote their songs based on personal experiences or testimonies. The songs were meant to encourage and give hope to people going through difficult situations. Hymns such as, "What A Friend We Have In Jesus," "Blessed Assurance," "Tis So Sweet to Trust in Jesus," etc. Of course, there's nothing wrong with the contemporary music of today, but there's just something about those "old" songs! Be Blessed!

Psalm 95:1-2

DAILY REFLECTIONS

APRIL 24

Despair

Anyone who has ever been addicted to caffeine is probably familiar with the withdrawal symptoms they get when they try to wean off it. They may experience headaches, irritability, fatigue, and many other ailments as a result of withdrawal from the caffeine. Ironically, even though most people don't realize it, they experience withdrawal symptoms, too, when they try to distance themselves from God. They may experience a loss of energy and enthusiasm along with an overwhelming sense of hopelessness and despair. Their quality of life changes dramatically because living outside the hedge of God's protection isn't really a pleasant way to live at all! God promises us "peace that surpasses all understanding," "safety in the shelter of His tabernacle," "beauty instead of ashes," "gladness instead of mourning," and "praise instead of a spirit of despair." So, who could ask for anything more? A life without God in it is not really living at all! Be Blessed!

Psalm 27:5; Isaiah 61:3; Philippians 4:7

DAILY REFLECTIONS

APRIL 25

Forgiveness

Often, we get into situations with people where they are not treating us fairly. However, as Christians, we are expected to take the high road. They may be the ones at fault, or we may be; it doesn't really matter. Whatever, the case, "if it is possible, as far as it depends on you, live at peace with everyone." Therefore, when you are wrong, be quick to admit it and apologize. But even if you are not wrong, be quick to forgive, knowing that sometimes you will have to be the bigger person and take the initiative to make the first move. God will honor your effort and reward you openly! Be Blessed!

Romans 12:18

DAILY REFLECTIONS

APRIL 26

No Fear in God

At certain times in our lives, we feel afraid and completely alone. But, God told Joshua, "Be strong and courageous! Do not be afraid or discouraged. For the Lord your God is with you wherever you go." With that kind of assurance, what more can you ask for? Be Blessed!

Joshua 1:9

DAILY REFLECTIONS

APRIL 27

Submission

We should try not to get upset when we don't get recognition or appreciation from people. The only thing that matters is if we do what is pleasing to God. We must remember that we don't work for man, but we work for the Lord. Therefore, everything we do should glorify God. So, remember, man's opinion doesn't matter, because only what we do for Christ will last! "Serve wholeheartedly, as if you were serving the Lord, not men, because you know that the Lord will reward everyone for whatever good he does." Be Blessed!

Ephesians 6:7-8

DAILY REFLECTIONS

APRIL 28

Patience

If patience is a virtue, then why do so many people lack it? Most people want everything right now. We don't want to wait for God's timing. We live in a microwave society; everything is done in five minutes. Well, some of us have had to learn the hard way that you can't hurry God! So, you might as well develop patience, because that's exactly what you're going to need to survive in this life! "Therefore, as God's chosen people, holy and dearly loved, clothe yourselves with compassion, kindness, humility, gentleness, and patience. Bear with each other and forgive whatever grievances you may have against one another. Forgive as the Lord forgave you. And over all these virtues, put on love, which binds them all together in perfect unity." Be Blessed!

Colossians 3:12-14

DAILY REFLECTIONS

APRIL 29

Strongholds

Do you find yourself going through the same trials over and over again? You sacrifice for years to get yourself out of debt only to find yourself back in debt again? You exercise discipline for months (maybe even years), to eat right and follow an exercise program to successfully shed those extra pounds you want to get rid of. Then you turn around and find yourself slipping back into old habits and gaining a significant portion of the weight back! Or you work hard trying to bring those things that are not of God (i.e., lust, fornication, adultery, etc.), under subjection, only to find yourself being tempted and falling short again and again. All of us have something we are battling with. But God knows our struggles, and He is standing there with open arms ready to receive us when we fall. "We fall down, but we get up." "The steps of a good man are ordered by the Lord: and He delighteth in his way. Though he fall, he shall not be utterly cast down: for the Lord upholdeth him with His hand. I have been young and now I am old; yet I have never seen the righteous forsaken, nor his seed begging bread."

Psalm 37:23-25

DAILY REFLECTIONS

APRIL 30

Facing Your Fears

Are you striving to be the best that you can be? Are you trying with all your might to reach your dreams? Or are you hiding behind your fears and insecurities? God did not bring you this far so your dreams would be deferred simply because you are paralyzed in fear! You must do as David did and confront your fears so you can be confident in the Lord and what He has called you to do. "The Lord is my light and my salvation—whom shall I fear? The Lord is the stronghold of my life—of whom shall I be afraid? When evil men advance against me to devour my flesh, when my enemies and my foes attack me, they will stumble and fall. Though an army besiege me, my heart will not fear; though war break out against me, even then will I be confident. One thing I ask of the Lord, this is what I seek: that I may dwell in the house of the Lord all the days of my life, to gaze upon the beauty of the Lord and to seek Him in His temple. For in the day of trouble He will keep me safe in His dwelling; He will hide me in the shelter of His tabernacle and set me high upon a rock." Therefore, there is no reason to fear because when you "humble yourselves before the Lord, He will lift you up." Be Blessed!

Psalm 27:1-5, James 4:10

DAILY REFLECTIONS

MAY 1

God's Enduring Power

The Apostle Paul asked God three times to remove the thorn that plagued him from his side. However, God's response was "My grace is sufficient for thee, for My power is made perfect in weakness." Which goes to show that God will not always remove us from a situation or get rid of what is ailing us. He will, however, give us the strength to endure whatever it is. Therefore, put your trust and your faith in the One who is "able to do exceeding abundantly above anything we can ever ask or imagine." Be Blessed!

2 Corinthians 7:8-9, Ephesians 3:20

DAILY REFLECTIONS

_____
_____
_____
_____
_____
_____
_____
_____

MAY 2

Opportunities

Most of us stay so busy we don't have time to enjoy life. We don't have time for our families, our friends, or even the things we used to enjoy doing. What is it that is keeping us so busy? More importantly, when this life is over, will it have been worth all of the missed opportunities? "There is a time for everything, and a season for every activity under heaven: a time to be born and a time to die, a time to plant and a time to uproot, a time to kill and a time to heal, a time to tear down and a time to build, a time to weep and a time to laugh, a time to mourn and a time to dance, a time to scatter stones and a time to gather them, a time to embrace and a time to refrain, a time to search and a time to give up, a time to keep and a time to throw away, a time to tear and a time to mend, a time to be silent and a time to speak, a time to love and a time to hate, a time for war and a time for peace. What does the worker gain from his toil? I have seen the burden God has laid on men. He has made everything beautiful in its time." So, slow down and take the time to enjoy God's wonderful gift of life! Be Blessed!

Ecclesiastes 3:1-11

DAILY REFLECTIONS

MAY 3

Truth Sets Us Free

2 Timothy 2:15 tells us to "study to show thyself approved"; therefore none of us should act like we know everything under the sun! Sometimes we get attitudes with people when they don't agree with us or see things the way we do. No one is right all the time, and a true friend will tell you the truth, even if it means you get mad at them. So, instead of getting upset when people don't agree with you, thank God for sending you friends that love you enough to be honest with you and tell you the truth! "Then you will know the truth, and the truth will set you free"! Be Blessed!

2 Timothy 2:15, John 8:32

DAILY REFLECTIONS

_____
_____
_____
_____
_____
_____
_____
_____
_____
_____

MAY 4

Love

John 3:16 is the scripture reference for the foundation of understanding the depth of God's love for us. "For God so loved the world that He gave His one and only Son, that whoever believe in Him shall not perish but have everlasting life." "No greater love has anyone than this; that He lay down His life for His friends." Be Blessed!

John 3:16, 15:13

DAILY REFLECTIONS

_____
_____
_____
_____
_____
_____
_____
_____
_____
_____

MAY 5

God's Promises of Double Blessings

When the stresses of life are weighing you down, don't get discouraged. The same God that made a way before can make a way this time, too! God knows your situation and will not put more on you than you can bear. So, don't let the enemy tempt you into giving up. God has not forgotten you! He has promised to give you double for your trouble, and "He is faithful that promised." "Instead of their shame my people will receive a double portion, and instead of disgrace they will rejoice in their inheritance; and so they will inherit a double portion in their land, and everlasting joy will be theirs." Be Blessed!

Isaiah 61:7, Hebrews 10:23

DAILY REFLECTIONS

MAY 6

In God's Presence

Sometimes senseless acts occur in our lives that we just don't understand. But that is the time when we have to turn to and put our faith and trust in the One who "is able to keep us from falling." "Now unto Him that able to keep you from falling, and to present you faultless before the presence of His glory with exceeding joy. To the only wise God our Savior, be glory and majesty, dominion and power, both now and ever. Amen.

Jude 1:24-25

DAILY REFLECTIONS

Financial Security

When major financial institutions file bankruptcy and others are bought out or require government bailouts, it is understandable for people to wonder about their future financial security. However, as a child of God, you know that "God shall supply all your need according to His riches in glory by Christ Jesus." But, you must do your part. You can't mismanage your money and then sit back and say, "God will provide." You have a responsibility to be a good steward over the money God has blessed you with. So, forget about what's happening on Wall Street and pay attention to what's happening on *your* street! Be Blessed!

Philippians 4:19

DAILY REFLECTIONS

MAY 7

Destiny

So many times we set goals or make plans for our lives without consulting God, and then we wonder why things don't work out. It is a waste of time to make plans without consulting God first because He knows what our lives are destined to be before we are even born! "All the days ordained for me were written in your book before one of them came to be." Therefore, our plans need to be in line with His so we can fulfill the purpose that God created us for! "In Him we were also chosen, having been predestined according to the plan of Him who works out everything in conformity with the purpose of His will." Be Blessed!

Psalm 139:16, Ephesians 1:11

DAILY REFLECTIONS

MAY 9

God Works it Out for Our Good

Although bad situations may come our way, God will work them out for our good. We often get upset when we have to go through difficulties, but that's what has to happen in order for the good to come out of it. No one said we have to enjoy the bad times; we just need to know they are necessary for us to get to the good times! "And we know that in all things God works for the good of those who love Him, who have been called according to His purpose." Be Blessed!

Romans 8:28

DAILY REFLECTIONS

MAY 10

Praise

"O Lord, our Lord, how excellent is Thy name in all the earth."
When I think of all the things that God has done in my life, I can't help but shout, Hallelujah! When you're going through a rough time in your life and things begin to look bleak, think on "whatever is true, whatever is noble, whatever is right, whatever is pure, whatever is lovely, whatever is admirable—if anything is excellent or praiseworthy—think about such things." Be Blessed!

Psalm 8:1, Philippians 4:8

DAILY REFLECTIONS

MAY 11

Loving Unconditionally

I thank God that we are "fearfully and wonderfully made." Even with all of our flaws, we can be thankful because God loves us unconditionally. We must learn to love ourselves and one another in the same manner that God loves us. We spend so much time being critical that we forget how blessed we truly are! The next time you find yourself starting to judge or criticize someone (even yourself), make a conscious decision to give a compliment instead. "Do not let any unwholesome talk come out of your mouths, but only what is helpful for building others up." Be Blessed!

Psalm 139:14, Ephesians 4:29

DAILY REFLECTIONS

MAY 12

Thankfulness

We must cherish each day that we are given, because having another day of life is truly a blessing. We take it for granted, but tomorrow is not promised to us. Therefore, count your blessings daily and thank God for what He has already done, for what He is doing right now, and for what He may do in the future, if we're blessed enough to see it. "My soul glorifies the Lord and my spirit rejoices in God my Savior, for He has been mindful of the humble state of His servant. From now on all generations will call me blessed, for the Mighty One has done great things for me—Holy is His Name." Be Blessed!

Luke 1:46-49

DAILY REFLECTIONS

_____
_____
_____
_____
_____
_____
_____
_____
_____

MAY 13

Mercy

Some people look at the number 13 as a "bad luck" number. But there are people who were born on the 13th, so how can it be bad luck? The gift of life is always a good thing! So, view today just like any other. Another day we've been given to bask in the glory and the gift of life that is filled with brand new mercies each and every day! "Yet this I call to mind and therefore I have hope: Because of the Lord's great love we are not consumed, for His compassions never fail. His mercies are new every morning; great is His faithfulness." Be Blessed!

Lamentations 3:21-23

DAILY REFLECTIONS

MAY 14

God's Amazing Power

Have you ever had something happen to you that you just couldn't believe? Like an impossible situation turning around for you in such a way that you knew it was nobody but God that could have done it? God promised David that He would make His enemies his footstool and that He would prepare a table for him in the presence of his enemies; and He will do the same for you! "Even though I walk through the valley of the shadow of death, I will fear no evil, for you are with me; your rod and your staff, they comfort me. You prepare a table before me in the presence of my enemies. You anoint my head with oil; my cup overflows. Surely goodness and mercy will follow me all the days of my life, and I will dwell in the house of the Lord forever." So, don't be surprised when miracles happen in your life; that's just God placing the enemy under your feet! Be Blessed!

Psalm 23:4-6

DAILY REFLECTIONS

MAY 15

Omnipotence

Occasionally, we get upset with God because things aren't turning out the way we planned. Although these may be normal emotions, they are slightly misdirected. Instead of getting upset with God, why not consider that it could be God trying to strengthen our faith, or maybe even the enemy trying to destroy it! We have to put things in the proper perspective so that we don't allow the circumstances to become the main focus. What we should be concentrating on is God's ability to handle it! Remember, no matter what the situation, God is able "to do exceeding abundantly above all that we ask or think." Be Blessed!

Ephesians 3:20

DAILY REFLECTIONS

MAY 16

Resting in God

Do you know how to enter into God's rest? The truth is most of us don't. We will encounter trials and tribulations throughout our entire life, that's a fact. The way we deal with them is what makes the difference. We can get stressed out and upset about them, but that won't change it. We can ignore it or deny its existence, but that won't change it either. What God wants us to do is trust Him in *all* things. He is in control and able to handle whatever we encounter. Therefore, put your trust in the One who knows all, is in all, and supplies all of our needs. If you learn to do that, you can enter into God's rest. "Do not be afraid. Stand firm and you will see the deliverance the Lord will bring you today…The Lord will fight for you; you need only to be still." Be Blessed!

Exodus 14:13-14

DAILY REFLECTIONS

MAY 17

Steadfastness

Keeping the faith is not always easy, especially when things aren't going as planned. You've been praying and fasting, but you still don't see a breakthrough. You're trying to hold on, but you don't know how much more you can bear. Although we know God's time is not our time, the wait still seems unbearable. What do you do while you're waiting for God's promise to come to pass? You remain "steadfast and unmovable, always abounding in the work of the Lord." "And the God of all grace, who called you to His eternal glory in Christ, after you have suffered a little while, will Himself restore you and make you strong, firm and steadfast." Be Blessed!

1 Corinthians 15:58, 1 Peter 5:10

DAILY REFLECTIONS

___
___
___
___
___
___
___
___
___

MAY 18

Blessing Others

God wants us to be on the lookout for people we can bless. We need to learn how to be compassionate. Being compassionate is hard because it requires a lot of patience, and most of us don't have that. We must learn to be better listeners. You never know how God may use your ears to be the sounding board for someone who just needs someone to listen. So, take the focus off yourself and your problems and make a difference in someone else's life. If you focus on meeting other people's needs, God will make sure your needs are met! "And my God will meet all your needs according to His glorious riches in Christ Jesus." So, take time today to show someone you are concerned about them and that you really care! Be Blessed!

Philippians 4:19

DAILY REFLECTIONS

MAY 19

Complete in Him

When people look at you, are they able to see the *real* you, or are they seeing the façade that you've created for them to see? "Man may look at the outside, but God looks at your heart." God already knows what's wrong with you; He just needs you to acknowledge it so He can heal you! Because God has given you a free will, if you choose to stay in your mess, He will allow you to stay there! But that is not His desire for you. God desires for you to enjoy life to the fullest. "I have come that they may have life, and have it to the full." "You will seek me and find me when you seek me with all your heart." So, seek Him with all your heart, so that His "joy may be in you and your joy may be complete." Be Blessed!

1 Samuel 16:7, John 10:10, Jeremiah 29:13, John 15:11

DAILY REFLECTIONS

MAY 20

Patience

So often when we pray, we want immediate results. But some of the things we are praying for won't happen overnight! We must exercise patience and endurance because Galatians 6:9 says, "Let us not become weary in doing good, for at the proper time we will reap a harvest if we do not give up." As we learn to wait on God, we will find that He will hear our cry and attend to our needs. "I waited patiently for the Lord; He turned to me and heard my cry. He lifted me out of the slimy pit, out of the mud and mire; He set my feet on a rock and gave me a firm place to stand. He put a new song in my mouth, a hymn of praise to our God. Many will see and fear and put their trust in the Lord. Blessed is the man who makes the Lord his trust." Be Blessed!

Galatians 6:9, Psalm 40:1-4

DAILY REFLECTIONS

MAY 21

The Power of Prayer

All of us have family members or friends that are struggling with one stronghold or another. Praying for someone's deliverance is not easy because they are often blocking their own blessing! We can pray and intercede on their behalf, but the ultimate decision to accept the deliverance is up to them. Although, *we* don't have the power to deliver them, God does. So, don't give up on them, keep on praying for them because "the effectual fervent prayer of a righteous man availeth much." Be Blessed!

James 5:16

DAILY REFLECTIONS

MAY 22

His Angels Are Watching Over You

When we go through our seasons of testing, it is very hard to hear God's voice because He is often silent during these times. But rest assured, He is still there watching and waiting to see what we are going to do. "Because God is our refuge, the High God our very own home, evil can't get close to us; harm can't get through the door. He ordered his angels to guard us wherever we go. If we stumble, they'll catch us; their job is to keep us from falling." Isn't it wonderful to know that even when we can't hear God's voice, we have the assurance that He has sent His angels to watch over us and protect us? Thank you, God, for your unfailing love! Be Blessed!

Psalm 91:9-12 (The Message Translation)

DAILY REFLECTIONS

MAY 23

Arrogance

Have you ever known someone who thought they knew everything? Who tried to be an authority on every subject and never thought they could be wrong about anything? Well, since the only person God created without a flaw was Jesus; people who think like that are misguided. The Bible says in Romans 12:3 not to "think of yourself more highly than you ought, but rather think of yourself with sober judgment, in accordance with the measure of faith God has given you." It also says in verse 16 not to be proud or conceited. Therefore, remember that "God opposes the proud but gives grace to the humble." Be Blessed!

Romans 12:3, 16, James 4:6

DAILY REFLECTIONS

MAY 24

Answered Prayer

We must learn to confess with our mouths whatever we believe God is bringing forth in our lives. For example, each time I pray, I thank God in advance for what I'm praying for. So, if I'm believing God to deliver me from depression, double-mindedness, a poverty mentality, and being true to His Word, my prayer should be something like this: "God, I thank you and praise you for joy unspeakable. I thank you for a faith that does not waver. I thank you for honoring your promises to me, and I thank you for supplying all of my needs! When you pray with confessions like that, you are not only telling God what your needs are, but you are thanking Him for them, which tells Him you trust Him and believe that He is going to honor your requests! Isn't it wonderful to be able to serve a God we know we can trust? "Praise be to the Lord, for He has heard my cry for mercy. The Lord is my strength and my shield; my heart trusts in Him, and I am helped." Be Blessed!

Psalm 28:6-7

DAILY REFLECTIONS

MAY 25

Procrastination

A lot of people struggle with procrastination, including me! The question is why do we do it? It only ends up frustrating us later on. It's funny how we have a hard time waiting on God, but we can wait forever to do the things we *need* to do! God's timing is always right. He's never late and He's never early. So, learn to trust in His timing and in His ways. "I had fainted, unless I had believed to see the goodness of the Lord in the land of the living. Wait on the Lord: be of good courage, and He shall strengthen thine heart: wait, I say, on the Lord." Be Blessed!

Psalm 27:13-14

DAILY REFLECTIONS

MAY 26

Love

Are you someone people can count on during trying times? Or are you a "fair weather friend?" God loves you through the good times and the bad and He expects you to do the same for others. "Therefore, as God's chosen people, holy and dearly loved, clothe yourselves with compassion, kindness, humility, gentleness and patience. Bear with each other and forgive whatever grievances you may have against one another. Forgive as the Lord forgave you. And over all these virtues put on love, which binds them all together in perfect unity." Be Blessed!

Colossians 3:12-14

DAILY REFLECTIONS

MAY 27

Obeying God's Commands

We should put into practice the saying, "if you can't say something nice, don't say anything at all." But unfortunately, we say terrible things to those closest to us! We don't honor our fathers and mothers and we say mean and degrading things to our children. We do this because of hurtful things that have been done or said to us in the past, because hurt people, HURT people. But we can break the cycle if we live what God's Word says, "Children, obey your parents because you belong to the Lord, for this is the right thing to do. "Honor your father and mother. This is the first of the Ten Commandments that ends with a promise. And this is the promise: If you honor your father and mother, "you will live a long life, full of blessing. And now a word to you fathers. Don't make your children angry by the way you treat them. Rather, bring them up with the discipline and instruction approved by the Lord." So, don't worry about what was done to you, Psalm 27:10 says, "though my father and mother forsake me, the Lord will receive me." So, even if your parents didn't do right by you, if you do your part, the Lord will do the rest! Be Blessed!

Ephesians 6:1-4, Psalm 27:10

DAILY REFLECTIONS

_____
_____
_____
_____
_____
_____
_____
_____
_____

MAY 28

All is Well

2 Kings 4:8-37 tells the story of a woman whom the prophet Elisha told would have a son. A year later she did have the son that Elisha had prophesied to her about. Some years later, however, the son died. This did not sit well with the woman at all! She would not accept that God would bless her with this miracle child and then take him away. So, she went to find Elisha, in order to have him honor his prophecy and promise to her. She would not accept anything other than her son's healing, so whenever anybody asked her about it, she would say, "all is well." She found Elisha and brought him back to her house. Elisha prayed to God and was able to bring her son back to life. We need to have the same attitude that the woman from Shunem had! Whatever circumstances come our way, we have to remember that God is in control and that "all things will work together for our good." Therefore, we can also say, "all is well," because we know that God is faithful and "His Word does not return to Him void." So, as you go about facing life's challenges, remember, no matter what it looks like, "*All is well*!" Be Blessed!

2 Kings 4:8-37, Romans 8:28, Isaiah 55:11

DAILY REFLECTIONS

MAY 29

Conquering Fear

What is keeping you from reaching your destiny? Is it fear? Is it some kind of addiction or bad habit? Or have you allowed your circumstances to limit you? Whatever it is, you must choose to overcome it! God did not create you with a purpose and destiny in mind just to set you up for failure. Therefore, you can step out on faith knowing you will succeed. "Commit to the Lord whatever you do, and your plans will succeed. The Lord works out everything for His own ends." Be Blessed!

Proverbs 16:3-4

DAILY REFLECTIONS

MAY 30

Rest

Have you ever been so tired that you couldn't even sleep? Thoughts keep running through your mind reminding you about things you need to do? It is very stressful when you juggle too many tasks. You'll find that you don't even have time to enjoy life. So, slow down, relax, and breathe. "When you lie down, you will not be afraid; when you lie down, your sleep will be sweet. Have no fear of sudden disaster or of the ruin that overtakes the wicked, for the Lord will be your confidence and will keep your foot from being snared." Be Blessed!

Proverbs 3:24-26

DAILY REFLECTIONS

MAY 31

Confronting Your Strongholds

Have you ever found yourself faced with the same issues over and over again? Do you know why? It could be you haven't learned the lesson so you continue to go through it again and again until you decide to do something different to change the situation. Or it can be because you refuse to confront the issues in your life, so you continue to stay stuck in the mess and eventually get comfortable with the dysfunction. It's time, however, for you to do something different! It is said that doing the same thing over and over again but expecting different results is insanity. So, you need to make up your mind to deal with your "stuff" and stop letting your "stuff" deal with you! God is in control and He will not let any harm come near you. Therefore, the Word of God says, "Fear not, for I have redeemed you; I have summoned you by name; you are mine. When you pass through the waters, I will be with you; and when you pass through the rivers, they will not sweep over you. When you walk through the fire, you will not be burned; the flames will not set you ablaze. For I am the Lord, your God, the Holy One of Israel, your Savior." Be Blessed!

Isaiah 43:1-3

DAILY REFLECTIONS

JUNE 1

Worship and Praise

" Taste and see that the Lord is good; blessed is the man that takes refuge in Him." Because "God is our refuge and strength, and an ever-present help in trouble; we don't have to fear." I'm so glad I serve a God who is everything I need, and everything I am. He is the Almighty God, the Everlasting Father, the Prince of Peace, the Wonderful Counselor, and the "Lifter of my Head." I love you and adore you, Lord, and I will place no one before you. "The Heavens declare your glory"; honor and praise belong to you and you only. I worship you just because of who you are! Thank you, Lord, for being my all and all!

Psalms 3:3, 19:1, 34:8, 46:1-2, Isaiah 9:6

DAILY REFLECTIONS

JUNE 2

Power of God

There's nothing like having an intimate relationship with God. You can go to Him anytime and anywhere and know that He will hear your cry and attend to your need. Because of God's omnipotence, He can do "exceeding abundantly above all that we could ever ask or think." So, whether your problems are big or small, God is concerned about them and wants to deliver you from them all. Therefore, be assured that you can take your burdens to the Lord and leave them there! "Give your burdens to the Lord, and He will take care of you. He will not permit the godly to slip and fall." Be Blessed!

Ephesians 3:20, Psalm 55:22

DAILY REFLECTIONS

JUNE 3

Reconciliation

Do you find yourself singing the same old song to God? Why God Why? When God When? Where God Where? Well, it's time to "sing unto the Lord a *new* song." "Sing unto the Lord a new song; for He hath done marvelous things." God wants to do a new thing in you. Will you let go of the old stuff so He can do it? "What this means is that those who become Christians become new persons. They are not the same anymore, for the old life is gone. A new life has begun! All this newness of life is from God, who brought you back to Himself through what Christ did. And God has given you the task of reconciling people to Him. For God was in Christ, reconciling the world to Himself, no longer counting people's sins against them. This is the wonderful message He has given you to tell others. You are Christ's ambassadors, and God is using you. I urge you, as though Christ Himself were here pleading with you, "Be reconciled to God." For God made Christ, who never sinned, to be the offering for your sin, so that you could be made right with God through Christ." Be Blessed!
        Psalm 98:1, 2 Corinthians 5:17-21 (New Living Translation)

DAILY REFLECTIONS

JUNE 4

Rest in God

When we allow our bodies to get run down, we will become weary; not only in body, but also in spirit. It is during these times that the enemy will attack us because he knows we're worn down. That is why it is so important to stay prayed up, physically fit, and in control of our lives. Don't worry, though. We don't have to do it all by ourselves. Our Heavenly Father is right there with open arms waiting for us to rest in Him. "Come to me, all you who are weary and burdened, and I will give you rest. Take my yoke upon you and learn from me, for I am gentle and humble in heart, and you will find rest for your souls. For my yoke is easy and my burden is light." So, stop loading yourself down with all those heavy burdens! Take your burdens to the Lord and leave them there! Be Blessed!

Matthew 11:28-30

DAILY REFLECTIONS

Spiritual Warfare

Everyone I know is in a spiritual battle right now, including me! It's no doubt that the enemy is mad about God's children being saved. But he's even more upset that we are reaching back to help others get saved, too! He wasn't worried when we were just going to church and continuing to live the same old lives. But when we started getting in right relationship with God and started changing our lives, the devil started to lose his mind! He wasn't about to stand for that, and that's when he started wreaking havoc in our lives. Jesus already defeated the devil, so he has no real power over us. We just have to take the authority given us through Jesus Christ and put him under our feet! We cannot be passive about it, though, because our very lives are at stake! We need to put on the whole armor of God that Paul speaks about in Ephesians 6. We must take it up and put it on *every* day, so we are protected when the enemy comes. He is not playing with us, so we need to stop playing with him! "Finally, my brethren, be strong in the Lord, and in the power of His might. Put on the whole armor of God, so that you will be able to stand firm against all the strategies and tricks of the devil." Remember, in the end, we win! So, put on that armor and *fight*. Be Blessed!

Ephesians 6:10-18 (King James and New Living Translation Versions)

DAILY REFLECTIONS

JUNE 6

Surrender

Has God ever kept you in a "holding pattern?" A "holding pattern" is a span of time, in which you are held while you are waiting for God to move in your life. I would venture to say it is not a scary place to be in, nor is it anything to be anxious about. But it can be a very frustrating place to be in! I've been in several "holding patterns" in my life! However, I have learned that it is during these times that God is pruning you, maturing you, training you, and delivering you. It is necessary for you to go through this in order to prepare you for where He's taking you. So, I don't fight it anymore when I'm in a "holding pattern" because I realize it is just a test. But you must pass the test before God can promote you to the next level. So, stop delaying your promotion by trying to fight God's plan for your life. "Your arm's too short to box with God." Therefore, submit your will, and surrender to His! You'll be glad you did! "Delight Yourself in the Lord, and He Will Give You the Desires of Your Heart." Be Blessed!

Psalm 37:4

DAILY REFLECTIONS

JUNE 7

Good Example

One of the ways a parent knows if they have done a good job raising their kids is watching to see what they will do when they are away from them. Will they exercise good behavior like they have been taught, or will they embarrass their parents by acting as if they have had no "home training?" I know that was one of my parents' famous lines when we were going to other people's homes, "Don't go out here acting like you don't have any home training." They wanted to make sure we behaved well because if we didn't, it was a reflection on them! God feels the same way. If He has already given us the tools for righteous living, and sanctified us through the blood of Jesus Christ, there is no reason for us to be living unfulfilled and sinful lives! So, sometimes He will hold us in this testing period until we are ready to make Him a proud parent. The choice is up to us. Will we continue to "act out," or "step up?" God has already approved us for the next level. So, are we going to be willing to do what we need to do in order to go? "Blessed are those who hunger and thirst for righteousness, for they will be filled." Be Blessed!

Matthew 5:6

DAILY REFLECTIONS

JUNE 8

Jesus Christ is The Way

We can seek for happiness in riches in fame, people or places, but following Jesus is the only way to true happiness and everlasting joy. "Though you have not seen Him, you love Him; and even though you do not see Him now, you believe in Him and are filled with an inexpressible and glorious joy." Be Blessed!

1 Peter 1:8

DAILY REFLECTIONS

JUNE 9

Faith

Stepping out on faith is not always easy. Most of the time when God gives you a vision, you're the only one He has given it to. Therefore, people won't understand what you are doing, and there will be many naysayers who will try to discourage you. It's during this time that you will have to exercise your faith the most! "What is faith? It is the confident assurance that what we hope for is going to happen. It is the evidence of things we cannot yet see. God gave His approval to people in days of old because of their faith." Therefore, in order to step out in faith, you have to be willing to go forward even if you don't see how it's going to work out. "For we walk by faith, not by sight." So, go ahead, step out! Be Blessed!

Hebrews 11:1, 2 Corinthians 5:7

DAILY REFLECTIONS

JUNE 10

Guidance

Often in our lives we are faced with difficult decisions, and we don't know which way to turn. We go to people for advice, but we just get more confused! Because God knows all and is in all, we should go to Him for advice and instruction. James 1:5 says, "If any of you lacks wisdom, he should ask God." God knows what your future holds, so He will not lead you astray. "Trust in the Lord with all your heart and lean not on your own understanding; in all your ways acknowledge Him, and He will direct your paths." Be Blessed!

James 1:5, Proverbs 3:5-6

DAILY REFLECTIONS

JUNE 11

Prayer Time

As children, a lot of us were taught to say our prayers every night before going to bed. But as the years went by, our schedules got busier, we started families of our own, we stayed up late working on projects, we fell asleep watching TV, etc. As a result, our prayer before bedtime became almost non-existent. We justified it by saying, we pray in the shower, on the way to work, while we're in the car, while we're cleaning the house, etc. However, God wants our undivided attention whenever we talk to Him. He is worthy of our honor, glory, and praise, so why wouldn't He be worthy of our quality time? Don't get caught up in the time, place, or position, because some people may not be able to pray in the evening or have the ability to get down on their knees. The only thing that matters is that we set aside quality time each day to spend with God. How it's executed is between us and God. "Be joyful in hope, patient in affliction, faithful in prayer." Be Blessed!

Romans 12:12

DAILY REFLECTIONS

_____
_____
_____
_____
_____
_____
_____
_____
_____

JUNE 12

Good Example

We live in a society where we're taught to "look out for #1." However, this is not the example that Jesus set for us, nor the way that Paul described how we are supposed to be. "In everything set them an example by doing what is good." We are to set an example, but we are also advised not to do anything that will "cause our brother to stumble." "It is better not to eat meat or drink wine or to do anything else that will cause your brother to fall." Therefore, we must remember "God made him who had no sin to be sin for us, so that in Him we might become the righteousness of God." Not only for our sake, but also for those who will follow behind us. So, remember, when you're looking out for #1, nos. 2, 3, 4, 5, etc. are right behind you following your example! Be Blessed!

Titus 2:7, Romans 14;21, 2 Corinthians 5:21

DAILY REFLECTIONS

JUNE 13

Purpose

A friend gave me a book several years ago titled, *Sober, But Stuck*. At the time, I wondered why she gave me that book. She said it was because she could visualize where God was trying to take me, but I wasn't doing anything to help myself get there. The problem was I didn't know how to get there! So I asked God to show me His "good and perfect will" for my life, and He did. God will do the same thing for you, too! The challenge comes, however, when we try to get out of situations we are "stuck" in. The enemy doesn't just step aside and say, "Oh, I see God has a plan for your life, so let me get out of the way." Oh no, he does just the opposite! He begins to set strongholds in our mind to make us think that we will never be able to do what God has called us to do. That we will never be able to change, things will always be the same, we don't have what it takes, etc. But "the devil is a liar and the truth is not in him."

Romans 12:2, John 8:44, Philippians 1:6

DAILY REFLECTIONS

JUNE 14

God's Sovereignty

" Ah, Sovereign Lord, you have made the heavens and the earth by your great power and outstretched arm. "Nothing is too hard for you." When we think of God's almighty power and greatness, and all that He has done for us, we can't help but to stand in awe of Him! His Word says, "Nothing is too difficult for Him." So, what are worrying about? Whatever we are facing, we have the confidence of knowing God is able to handle it, because He's already proven that "nothing is impossible for Him." Be Blessed!

Jeremiah 32:7, Genesis 18:14, Luke 1:37

DAILY REFLECTIONS

JUNE 15

In His Safety

As kids, we used to play a game called "Hide and Seek." Some of us are still trying to play that game today! We put on facades for people, hoping they won't be able to find out who we really are. The scary thing is, if we hide behind our issues too long, we may lose sight of ourselves! God, however, has a different kind of hiding place for us. He has promised that "in the day of trouble He will keep us safe in His dwelling; He will hide us in the shelter of His tabernacle and set us high upon a rock." So, if you're looking for a place to hide, why not find shelter in the "shadow of the Almighty?" "If you make the Most High your dwelling...then no harm will befall you, no disaster will come near your tent. For He will command His angels concerning you to guard you in all your ways." Be Blessed!

Psalms 27:5, 91:1, 9-11

DAILY REFLECTIONS

JUNE 16

Changing Habits

If you've been trying to accomplish something but don't seem to be getting anywhere, then maybe it's time you tried doing something different. It has been said that insanity is doing the same thing over and over again but expecting a different outcome. Your circumstances will only change when you decide to do something different! "As a dog returns to its vomit, so a fool repeats his folly." Don't be like the dog or the fool. Make a commitment today to do something different so you can get the outcome you desire! Be Blessed!

Proverbs 26:11

DAILY REFLECTIONS

JUNE 17

Staying Joyful

When things go wrong in your life, how do you react? Do you have a pity party? Do you sulk and get mad? Do you have a temper tantrum? Hopefully, you don't do any of these things, because none of them will do you any good. Instead, you should continue to have a good attitude, even in the midst of tribulations. Paul advises us in James 1:2-4 to "Consider it pure joy, my brothers, whenever you face trials of many kinds, because you know that the testing of your faith develops perseverance. Perseverance must finish its work so that you may be mature and complete, not lacking anything." So, the next time you are faced with a challenge, instead of becoming anxious about it, "count it all joy." Be Blessed!

James 1:2-4

DAILY REFLECTIONS

JUNE 18

Live in Harmony

Do you ever find yourself getting upset or offended when people approach you about things? Do you have a reputation for being difficult to deal with? Have you ever been told that people avoid telling you things because they're afraid you'll "go off" on them? If so, you might want to work on that! You can't be a positive witness for Christ if people have a negative opinion of you. As a child of God, you should strive to be more like Jesus. "Live in harmony with one another. Do not be proud but be willing to associate with people of low position. Do not be conceited. Do not repay anyone evil for evil. Be careful to do what is right in the eyes of everybody. If it is possible, as far as it depends on you, live at peace with everyone." Be Blessed!

Romans 12:16-18

DAILY REFLECTIONS

JUNE 19

God's Mercy

Sometimes when you least expect it, God will bless you in a supernatural way to remind you just how good He is! "O give thanks unto the Lord; for He is good; for His mercy endureth forever." Be Blessed!

I Chronicles 16:34

DAILY REFLECTIONS

JUNE 20

Forgiveness

Resentment is a wasted emotion that drains your spirit and zaps your strength. Therefore, we must make it a habit not to harbor resentment against those who have wronged us or mistreated us. We must remember that people are only human and that "we all fall short of God's glory." Even at their best attempts, people will sometimes let us down. But God will "never leave us nor forsake us." Be Blessed!

Romans 3:23, Deuteronomy 31:6

DAILY REFLECTIONS

JUNE 21

Mentoring Others

Sometimes God allows us to experience situations in our lives so we are prepared to assist others when the same thing happens to them. Instead of being bitter about the situations we went through, use them as opportunities to bless someone else. Who can better minister to someone going through a divorce than a divorcee? A person who has recovered from substance abuse addiction would be an excellent Substance Abuse Counselor because they've already experienced everything their clients are going to go through. You can relate better to something you've already experienced than something you know nothing about. Therefore, don't look at your circumstances as burdensome, but as future opportunities to bless someone else with the knowledge you gained from your experience that is going to help them overcome theirs! "You intended to harm me, but God intended it for good to accomplish what is now being done, the saving of many lives." Be Blessed!

Genesis 50:20

DAILY REFLECTIONS

JUNE 22

Stress Free Living

So often we get burnt out in our Christian walk because we try to do things on our own. But God never intended for us to go it alone! Stop stressing and wearing yourself out trying to do something you can't do. Let Go and Let God! He is more than able to see you through whatever it is you're going through! "I can do all things through Christ who strengthens me." Be Blessed!

Philippians 4:13

DAILY REFLECTIONS

JUNE 23

God is Our Refuge

Whenever we are faced with challenges in life, we must learn where to go to find refuge. "God is our refuge and strength, a very present help in trouble." So often we try superficial means to get us through hard times, such as drugs, alcohol, food, work, sex, etc. But those are just temporary fixes. Nothing can heal our hurts, but God. Nothing can calm our fears, but God. Nothing can deliver us from temptation, but God. Nothing can provide for our *every* need, but God! So, why go anywhere else? "I will lift up mine eyes unto the hills, from whence cometh my help. My help cometh form the Lord." Be Blessed!

Psalm 46:1, 121:1

DAILY REFLECTIONS

JUNE 24

One Day at a Time

" One Day At A Time" was a favorite gospel song of one of my uncles. That song has helped me put things into perspective on many a day! I especially like the stanza that says:

> "Yesterday's gone, sweet Jesus,
> And tomorrow may never be mine
> Lord, for my sake, help me to take,
> One Day At A Time."

We should always live each day to the fullest, because tomorrow is not promised to us. Don't take one moment for granted, because as we see every day on the news, we may never get another chance to tell or show our loved ones that we love them. We can be here one minute and gone the next. "Therefore keep watch, because you do not know the day or the hour." Be Blessed!

Matthew 25:13

DAILY REFLECTIONS

_____
_____
_____
_____
_____
_____
_____
_____

JUNE 25

Sowing Good Seeds

When you're going through your toughest times, that's the time to sow a seed into someone else's life. When we stay focused on our problems, they just get bigger and bigger. But, when we take time to be a blessing to someone else, it takes our mind off ourselves. "Whoever sows sparingly will also reap sparingly, and whoever sows generously will also reap generously. Each man should give what he has decided in his heart to give, not reluctantly or under compulsion, for God loves a cheerful giver. And God is able to make all grace abound to you, so that in all things at all times, having all that you need, you will abound in every good work." Be Blessed!

2 Corinthians 9:6-8

DAILY REFLECTIONS

JUNE 26

God is With Us Always

God is truly amazing! Even when we have our bad days, we have His assurance that He is right there with us. Jesus was with the disciples in their storm, and God is with us in ours. "Surely I am with you always. To the very end of the age." Be Blessed!

Matthew 28:20

DAILY REFLECTIONS

_____
_____
_____
_____
_____
_____
_____
_____
_____

JUNE 27

Spiritual Gifts

Because God has given each of us gifts and talents, we should desire to find out what our calling is, and then begin to operate in it if we're not already doing so. "We have different gifts, according to the grace given us." It would be a shame for us to die with our "gifts" still in us! So, determine today to find out what God has destined for you to do and then begin blessing others by doing it! Be Blessed!

Romans 12:6

DAILY REFLECTIONS

JUNE 28

The Battle is The Lord's

We are faced with things we have to battle every day. We are struggling in our relationships, our children are acting out in school, our parents are aging, and we don't know what to do. The first thing we must remember is God is greater than any problem we face. He is also ready and willing to fight all our battles for us. Therefore, we don't have to fight them by ourselves. God has promised to fight our battles for us. "Do not be afraid or discouraged because of this vast army. For the battle is not yours, but God's." Be Blessed!

2 Chronicles 20:15

DAILY REFLECTIONS

___
___
___
___
___
___
___
___
___

JUNE 29

God's Grace

We deceive ourselves when we fail to confront the issues in our lives. Nothing in our lives will ever change until we are honest with ourselves and face the truth. We're not perfect, and God doesn't expect us to be. But until we acknowledge we have strongholds in our lives, God will not tear them down. He is a gracious God, and He will not force himself or His deliverance on us. It is up to us to want to make a change. If we make an honest effort to change, He will honor our effort and attend to our cry. "Humble yourselves before the Lord, and He will lift you up." Praise be to the Lord, for He has heard my cry for mercy. The Lord is my strength and my shield; my heart trusts in Him, and I am helped." Be Blessed!

James 4:10, Psalm 28:6-7

DAILY REFLECTIONS

JUNE 30

The Love of God

If we followed the example of Jesus, we would have no problem loving one another. However, we become so focused on judging people, that we forget to love them. God loves us unconditionally, faults and all. Wouldn't it be wonderful if we did the same? "May your unfailing love be with us, Lord, even as we put our hope in you." Be Blessed!

Psalm 33:22

DAILY REFLECTIONS

JULY 1

Abundant Life

The walls that we build around ourselves to protect us from getting hurt, are the same walls that will shut God out, too. The need to protect ourselves from getting hurt is understandable, but we must realize it is very unrealistic. The truth of the matter is, in this life we will get hurt because life is full of disappointments! However, the good news is we serve a God who is able to see us through those hurts and disappointments. We bring needless pain and suffering on ourselves by living in fear and denying ourselves the abundant life Jesus died to give us. The devil doesn't want us to have that joy, so he will keep us in bondage for as long as we let him. But Jesus died so we would have the victory over Satan. Always remember what Jesus said, "the thief comes only to steal and kill and destroy; but I have come that you might have life and that more abundantly." Be Blessed!

John 10:10

DAILY REFLECTIONS

JULY 2

Fellowship

Have you heard the expression, "No man is an island?" We were not created to be separate from each other, yet so many people seclude themselves from the world because of their fears of being hurt. When God created the earth, He looked around and decided that "it is not good for man to be alone" and He created a mate for Adam. Whether it is with a mate or a circle of friends, God created us for fellowship and when we try to live outside the realm of our created purpose, we are out of order. Whenever we are out of order or outside of the will of God, we will not be at peace. So, why not get in line with God's will for our lives and enjoy life to the fullest? "Two are better than one, because they have a good return for their work: If one falls down, his friend can help him up. But pity the man who falls and has no one to help him up." If we make God our friend, we can rest assured that He's always "got our back" and will be there to catch us when we fall! "Though he stumble, he will not fall, because the Lord upholds him with His hand." Be Blessed!

Genesis 2:18, Ecclesiastes 4:9-10, Psalm 37:24

DAILY REFLECTIONS

JULY 3

Faith

So many of us are operating in fear and don't even know it. Fear is the opposite of faith, but it is the same as unbelief. Therefore, if we are afraid, we are saying we don't believe God will do what He said He would do. Hebrews 11:6 says, "Without faith it is impossible to please the Lord." So, if we want to live a life that is pleasing to the Lord, we must walk in faith, not fear. So when the enemy comes with his lies, we must cast them down! If he says, we're not good enough, tell him "he is a liar and the truth is not in him." When God created the earth, "He saw all that He had done and said it was *good*." So, who are we to go against what God said? "If God is for us, who can be against us?" Be Blessed!

Hebrews 11:6, John 8:44, Genesis 1:31, Romans 8:31

DAILY REFLECTIONS

JULY 4

Freedom

Each year we celebrate Independence Day as a reminder of the freedom we have here in the United States. It is a wonderful privilege so many people take for granted. We can look all around us and see other countries that are still operating under an oppressive government system. So, it is truly a blessing to live in a country where we are free. "Blessed is he whose help is the God of Jacob, whose hope is in the Lord his God, the Maker of heaven and earth, the sea, and everything in them—the Lord, who remains faithful forever. He upholds the cause of the oppressed and gives food to the hungry. The Lord sets prisoners free." Therefore, let us be grateful for the freedom we have not only in the United States, but more importantly, in Jesus Christ! Be Blessed!

Psalm 146:5-7

DAILY REFLECTIONS

JULY 5

Trusting God

So many times we ask God for things, but then we try to control how He will bring them to pass. God is a Sovereign God and He doesn't need our help in getting things done. He is omnipotent and omniscient, and He has His own way of doing things. We may want things to happen in a certain way, but that may not be the way God wants to do it. Ultimately, we must realize He knows what is best for us and trust Him to do what He needs to do in order to bring to pass. "Trust in the Lord and do good; dwell in the land and enjoy safe pasture. Delight yourself in the Lord and He will give you the desires of your heart. Commit your way to the Lord; trust in Him and He will do this." Be Blessed!

Psalm 37:3-5

DAILY REFLECTIONS

_____
_____
_____
_____
_____
_____
_____
_____
_____
_____

JULY 6

Humility

There are many things in life that can push your buttons if you let them. However, what good would that do if you let that happen? "Everyone should be quick to listen, slow to speak and slow to become angry, for man's anger does not bring about the righteous life that God desires. Therefore, get rid of all moral filth and the evil that is so prevalent and humbly accept the word planted in you, which can save you. Do not merely listen to the word, and so deceive yourselves. Do what it says." Be Blessed!

James 1:19-22

DAILY REFLECTIONS

God is in Control

There will be days when you just can't seem to get it together. However, those are the days when you need to take a minute and just breathe! It took God six days to finish His creation, so why would you think you could finish yours in one? You have your whole life to accomplish whatever it is God has purposed you to do. Therefore, stop putting pressure on yourself and just relax! God has it all under control! "For I know the plans I have for you," declares the Lord, "plans to prosper you and not to harm you, plans to give you hope and a future." "The plans of the Lord stand firm forever." Be Blessed!

Jeremiah 29:11, Psalm 33:11

DAILY REFLECTIONS

JULY 8

Victorious

Sometimes we face challenges in life that we just can't seem to overcome. We get discouraged and feel defeated, and oftentimes just want to give up. However, we must remember trials only come to make us stronger. Therefore, we can't give up because we've got to keep on getting stronger in the Lord! That is the only way we defeat the enemy. We can't defeat him in our own strength, but the good news is, we don't have to. "Thanks be to God! He gives us the victory through our Lord Jesus Christ. Therefore, my dear brothers, stand firm. Let nothing move you. Always give yourselves fully to the work of the Lord, because you know that your labor in the Lord is not in vain." So, stop trying to beat him in your own strength and lean on the everlasting arms of the Lord! Be Blessed!

1 Corinthians 15:57-58

DAILY REFLECTIONS

Conquering Fears

I'm sure we've all had something that we've been afraid of at one time or another. But what it is that we're afraid of? Is it the mere thought of it, or have we had a bad experience in the past? For example, many people are afraid of being hurt in relationships because they had a bad experience in the past. However, some people are just afraid of the possibility of it happening! They've never even had anything happen to them, yet they are allowing the fear of it to keep them from taking a chance at true happiness. There will always be a chance of something not turning out the way we planned. But if we never step out in faith and give it a try, we'll never experience the joy we could have if it did turn out the way we planned! Even if we step out and it doesn't work out, it is not the end of the world! We can still wake up tomorrow morning knowing God still loves us and has it all under control. "May your unfailing love be my comfort." So, start that business, follow that dream, or fall in love because life is too short to be afraid to take chances! "The Lord is my light and my salvation— whom shall I fear? The Lord is the stronghold of my life—of whom shall I be afraid?" Be Blessed!

Psalms 27:1, 119:76

DAILY REFLECTIONS

JULY 10

God's Presence

So many times when we go through hard times we feel alone and as if God is far away. We may even ask, "God, why did you leave me at a time when I needed you the most?" However, we can rest assured that God will never leave us! We may feel alone and dejected, but that is not God's doing. God promised "never to leave or forsake us." Therefore, we can put our trust in the one who "supplies all of our needs" and "sticks closer than a brother." "The Lord is a refuge for the oppressed, a stronghold in times of trouble. Those who know your name will trust in you, for you, Lord, have never forsaken those who seek you." So, if we want to feel God's presence when we're in trouble, call out to Him and watch Him come to the rescue. "God is our refuge and strength, an *ever-present* help in trouble." Be Blessed!

Deuteronomy 31:8, Joshua 1:5, Philippians 4:19, Proverbs 18:24, Psalms 9:9-10, 46:1

DAILY REFLECTIONS

JULY 11

Perseverance

So often when we have obstacles in our lives, we tend to focus on the difficulty of them instead of overcoming them. It's during those times that we need an attitude adjustment. We will encounter obstacles as long as we are on this earth. However, we must begin to see beyond the obstacles and keep our eyes on the prize. "I press on to take hold of that for which Christ Jesus took hold of me. Brothers, I do not consider myself yet to have taken hold of it. But one thing I do: Forgetting what is behind and straining toward what is ahead, I press on toward the goal to win the prize for which God has called me heavenward in Christ Jesus." Be Blessed!

Philippians 3:12-14

DAILY REFLECTIONS

JULY 12

God's Assurance

How well do you deal with change? Is it something you resist? Do you take it in stride? Or do you avoid it at all costs? Well, no matter how you answered those questions, one thing is certain; change will occur! Since it's going to happen anyway, you might as well be prepared for it. Your attitude in how you deal with it makes all the difference. You have God's assurance, though, that even when things in your life change, God will still remain the same. You can count on Him no matter what. "For I am the Lord, I change not." Thank you, Lord, for being a God who remains constant in an ever-changing world! Be Blessed!

Malachi 3:6, Hebrews 13:8

DAILY REFLECTIONS

JULY 13

Praise

In the midst of trying times, have you ever tried stopping and taking a "praise break?" Most people tend to stay focused on the situation, but that's just a trick of the enemy. If you continue to dwell on everything that is wrong in your life, you'll miss out on all that is good! So, try something different and begin to praise God, even during the storm! "I will praise you, O Lord, with all my heart; I will tell of all your wonders. I will be glad and rejoice in you; I will sing praise to your name, O Most High." So go on, and get your praise on! Be Blessed!

Psalm 9:1-2

DAILY REFLECTIONS

JULY 14

God's Direction

We are often faced with decisions that can change the course of our lives. Decisions that are difficult or maybe even seem impossible. But we must remember that "all things are possible with God." So, if we take our concerns to Him, He will direct our steps. "Show me your ways, O Lord, teach me your paths; guide me in your truth and teach me, for you are God my Savior, and my hope is in you all day long." Be Blessed!

Matthew 19:26, Psalm 25:4-5

DAILY REFLECTIONS

JULY 15

Unspeakable Joy

How can we attain this "inexpressible and glorious joy" that is described in 1 Peter 1:8? By immersing ourselves in God's Word, delighting ourselves in Him, and focusing on the goodness of the Lord in the land of the living! Oftentimes when we find ourselves in a struggle to stay optimistic, it is because we are not focusing on positive things. Instead of concentrating on our disappointments, we need to renew our minds to stay focused on God and the mighty things He has already done in our lives. The enemy doesn't want us to remember those blessings; instead he tries to keep us dwelling on the negative. So, when he comes at us with those fiery darts, we must cast them down and replace them with the truth of God's Word and the evidence of His love for us. "We demolish arguments and every pretension that sets itself up against the knowledge of God, and we take captive every thought to make it obedient to Christ." "Greater love has no one than this that He lay down His life for His friends." Be Blessed!

1 Peter 1:8, 2 Corinthians 10:5, John 15:13

DAILY REFLECTIONS

JULY 16

Trustworthy

I've heard the saying "Word is Bond" many times. It means whatever that person says can be trusted. They are staking their reputation on their word. Can that be said about you? Are you a person of integrity who can be trusted to keep their word? Not everyone can answer yes to that question, and if you are someone who cannot, then I pray you will ask God to help you improve in that area. Being a person of integrity is critical as a Christian because you are a child of the King! Children are a reflection of their parents, therefore, if you can't be trusted to keep your word that is a reflection on God. "When God made His promise to Abraham, since there was no one greater for Him to swear by, He swore by Himself, saying, "I will surely bless you and give you many descendants." And so after waiting patiently, Abraham received what was promised. Men swear by someone greater than themselves, and the oath confirms what is said and puts an end to all argument. Because God wanted to make the unchanging nature of His purpose very clear to the heirs of what was promised, *He confirmed it with an oath*. God did this so that, by two unchangeable things in which *it is impossible for God to lie*, we who have fled to take hold of the hope offered to us may be greatly encouraged." Therefore, since God's Word is Bond, yours should be too! Be Blessed!

Hebrews 6:13-18

DAILY REFLECTIONS

JULY 17

Forgiveness

We are often our own worst enemy. We're harder on ourselves than we are on anybody else. So, when we make a mistake, it is hard for us to forgive ourselves, too! However, God loved us so much that He sent His Son as an atonement for our sins. "This is how God showed His love among us: He sent His one and only Son into the world that we might live through Him. This is love: not that we loved God, but that He loved us and sent His Son as an atoning sacrifice for our sins." Therefore, since God has forgiven us, we must learn to forgive ourselves. Be Blessed!

1 John 4:9-11

DAILY REFLECTIONS

Trusting God

There will be times in your life when you will be faced with making moral decisions. This is not the time to try and do things on your own. God is willing and able to help you make the right choices. All you have to do is ask. The problem is most of the time people try to figure things out on their own without consulting God and then turn to Him when things go wrong. However, you don't have to make that mistake. You can seek God first and ask for His direction. He will never steer you wrong. "Trust in the Lord with all your heart and lean not on your own understanding; in all your ways acknowledge Him, and He will make your paths straight. Do not be wise in your own eyes; fear the Lord and shun evil." If you trust Him and never doubt, He will always bring you out! Be Blessed!

Proverbs 3:5-8

DAILY REFLECTIONS

JULY 19

Rejoice

"This is the day the Lord has made. Let us rejoice and be glad in it." Sometimes we have to make a choice to rejoice and be glad. Not too many of us wake up in a good mood *every* day. We will *all* have a bad day every now and then, no matter how positive we are. But in spite of all that, we can still choose to have joy. Who would prefer to stay grumpy and sad when they can be happy and glad? Remember, "The joy of the Lord is our strength." So, even if it's raining outside, the sun can still shine on the inside of us! Therefore, no matter what the weather looks like outside, or what bills may be due, or which co-worker may pluck my last nerve today, on *this* day, I will choose to rejoice and be glad in it! Be Blessed!

Nehemiah 8:10, Psalm 118:24

DAILY REFLECTIONS

Restoration

Some things will happen to us in life that will knock the very wind out of us! But instead of performing man's CPR (Cardiopulmonary Resuscitation), we should summon God's CPR (His Comfort, Protection, and Restoration). Cardiopulmonary Resuscitation will help to keep oxygen flowing and blood circulating until breathing and heart beat are restored. However, God's CPR restores our mind, body and spirit after the trials and tribulations of life have knocked us down and worn us out. "We are hard pressed on every side, but not crushed; perplexed, but not in despair; persecuted, but not abandoned; struck down, but not destroyed." When we feel persecuted, full of despair and abandoned, God is the Comforter who Protects us and Restores our joy. So, even though we might feel like giving up, quitting is not an option! God brought us out before, and He will do it again! Be Blessed!

2 Corinthians 4:8-9

DAILY REFLECTIONS

JULY 21

Striving for Excellence

Perfection is <u>not</u> something you should expect from yourself or from others. You should try to operate in a spirit of excellence, of course, always being mindful to take pride in all that you say and do. However, expecting perfection is unattainable, unrealistic and unnecessarily stressful. You should strive to be more like Jesus (who was perfection), and in doing so you will receive your just reward. "Whatever you do, work at it with all your heart, as working for the Lord, not for men, since you know that you will receive an inheritance from the Lord as a reward. It is the Lord Christ you are serving." Be Blessed!

Colossians 3:23-24

DAILY REFLECTIONS

JULY 22

Righteousness

Have you ever noticed that it costs more to eat healthy? It's as if you're being penalized for trying to eat right. It can feel like that sometimes on our Christian journey. We seem to struggle when those basking in sin appear to be having the time of their lives! But don't be fooled by appearances. Temporary pleasures cannot compare with eternal life! "Do not fret because of evil men or be envious of those who do wrong; for like the grass they will soon wither, like green plants they will soon die away. Trust in the Lord and do good; dwell in the land and enjoy safe pasture. Delight yourself in the Lord and He will give you the desires of your heart. Commit your way to the Lord; trust in Him and He will do this: He will make your righteousness shine like the dawn, the justice of your cause like the noonday sun. Be still before the Lord and wait patiently for Him; do not fret when men succeed in their ways, when they carry out their wicked schemes. Refrain from anger and turn from wrath; do not fret—it leads only to evil. For evil men will be cut off, but those who hope in the Lord will inherit the land. A little while, and the wicked will be no more; though you look for them, they will not be found. But the meek will inherit the land and enjoy great peace." Wait for it, for it will surely come! Be Blessed!

Psalm 37:1-12

DAILY REFLECTIONS

JULY 23

Priceless

I'm sure you've heard the saying, "anything worth having is worth fighting for," but it's also true that anything of value comes with a high price. Jesus paid a high price for you. He paid with His very life! That is an awesome testament of how valuable He thinks you are! Therefore, you should not take your life for granted and let Jesus' death be in vain. You are "fearfully and wonderfully made," so you need to start acting like it! "Do you not know that your body is a temple of the Holy Spirit, who is in you, whom you have received from God? You are not your own; you were bought at a price. Therefore, honor God with your body." He is worthy of all the praise, honor and glory. Be Blessed!

1 Corinthians 6:19-20, Psalm 139:14

DAILY REFLECTIONS

JULY 24

Stewardship

God desires for you to be a lender, not a borrower. Subsequently, He sent Paul, Silas, and Timothy to show us an example of being good, responsible stewards. "We were not idle when we were with you, nor did we eat anyone's food without paying for it. On the contrary, we worked night and day, laboring and toiling so that we would not be a burden to any of you. We did this, not because we do not have the right to such help, but in order to make ourselves a model for you to follow. For even when we were with you, we gave you this rule: "If a man will not work, he shall not eat." Therefore, follow their example and be a good steward of your money. Be Blessed!

Deuteronomy 28:12, 2 Thessalonians 3:7-10

DAILY REFLECTIONS

JULY 25

Fulfillment

A woman gives birth in the ninth month and a woman must go through labor before she gives birth. A baby resides in its mother's womb in an amniotic sac. At the time of delivery the amniotic sac is broken, or as more commonly termed, "her water breaks." A baby must be delivered soon after the mother's water breaks because they become susceptible to all kinds of attacks of infections and diseases. Some of you have been pregnant with a promise from God, and the enemy has been trying to attack you with all kinds of infections and diseases, so he can abort the promises of God over your life! But you can't let him do that! It is time for you to give birth! Your water has broken, so you must deliver now. You can no longer let your fears and doubts stop you! God gives you the promises, but you must make the choice to speak life to them. "I set before you life and death, blessing and cursing; therefore choose life, that both you and your descendants may life." So, go on give birth to the promises! Be Blessed!

Deuteronomy 30:19-20

DAILY REFLECTIONS

JULY 26

Love

Greek philosophers identify three aspects when defining love: *eros*, *philia*, and *agape*. *Eros* refers to the romantic or passionate love. *Philia* refers to friendships and loyal relationships, whereas, *agape* refers to the perfect kind of love; God's way of love without expectation of anything in return. 1 Corinthians 13:4-8 gives an even better definition: "Love is patient, love is kind. It does not envy, it does not boast, it is not proud. It is not rude, it is not self-seeking; it is not easily angered, it keeps no record of wrongs. Love does not delight in evil, but rejoices with the truth. It always protects, always trusts, always hopes, always perseveres. Love Never Fails." So, take a look at your "love walk," and see how you measure up. If you know you're not walking as you should, ask God to help you because there's no better teacher than the one who is love Himself. Be Blessed!

1 Corinthians 13:4-8

DAILY REFLECTIONS

JULY 27

Advocator

So often we beat ourselves up and feel guilty about mistakes from our past. However, we don't have to do that since Jesus died to free us from our sins. "My dear children, I write this to you so that you will not sin. But if anybody does sin, we have an advocate with the Father—Jesus Christ, the Righteous One. He is the atoning sacrifice for our sins, and not only for ours but also for the sins of the whole world." Thank You, Lord, for Jesus! Be Blessed!!!

1 John 2

DAILY REFLECTIONS

JULY 28

Worry

Whenever we find ourselves in a situation that we can't see any way out, remember "we walk by faith and not by sight." Don't get caught up in what the situation looks like, focus on who we know God to be; a faithful and all-powerful God. If we put our trust in Him, even though we can't see how, we can rest assured that He is working it out for our good. We must not empower the situation, but instead remember who has the power! God is bigger than any situation or circumstances, so we don't have to worry about it anymore, because "the battle is not ours, but the Lord's." Be Blessed!

2 Corinthians 5:7, 2 Chronicles 20:15

DAILY REFLECTIONS

JULY 29

God's Approval

Are you guilty of seeking others' approval, or trying to please or win their favor? If so, why are giving them that much power? Why does their opinion hold so much value? Ask yourself, "Am I now trying to win the approval of human beings, or of God? Or am I trying to please people?" If your answer is "yes," then you need to know the only approval you need to seek is God's. Be Blessed!

Galatians 1:10

DAILY REFLECTIONS

JULY 30

Motive

Sometimes you think you're doing the right thing, when actually you have an ulterior motive. "All a man's ways seem innocent to him, but motives are weighed by the Lord. Commit to the Lord whatever you do, and your plans will succeed." If you always remember to seek God first in all you do, then you eliminate the temptation to have selfish motives. You will know if your motives are selfish or not if you are looking for gratification or glory for yourself, instead of it all going to God. Remember, God is supposed to get the glory, not you! That was the cause of Satan's downfall; he wanted to get the glory instead of giving it to God. So be warned, "God will bring light to what is hidden in darkness, and will expose the motives of men's hearts." Be Blessed!

Proverbs 16:2, 1 Corinthians 4:5

DAILY REFLECTIONS

JULY 31

Faithfulness in the Midst of Trials

Oftentimes, we experience trials and tribulations in our lives and we begin to question God's faithfulness. We don't understand why God would allow something like this to happen to us. However, God did not stop loving us, providing for us, or taking care of us. Although troubling situations will happen in our lives, He is still there, and we can count on Him to be faithful as He always has been. So, hold onto your faith, and hold onto Him! "Know therefore that the Lord your God is God; He is the faithful God, keeping His covenant of love to a thousand generations of those who love Him and keep His commandments." Be Blessed!

Deuteronomy 7:9

DAILY REFLECTIONS

AUGUST 1

Worthiness

When I think of all of the wonderful things God does for us, my mind often wonders why He does it when we are so unworthy? However, it doesn't really matter why He does it; we just need to celebrate the fact that He does! "How awesome are your deeds! So great is your power that your enemies cringe before you. All the earth bows down to you; they sing praise to you, they sing praise to your name." Selah, Come and see what God has done, how awesome His works in man's behalf!" Thank you, Lord, for blessing us even in our unworthiness! Be Blessed!

Psalm 66:3-5

DAILY REFLECTIONS

AUGUST 2

Insecurity

People have insecurities about a number of things. We're insecure about our looks, material possessions, jobs, status, position, or even about how we feel about ourselves. But believe it or not, some of the richest, finest, popular, and successful people are the most insecure people in the world! Unless Christ is in our lives (in an up close and personal way), our lives are going to be empty. If we spend our lives trying to seek other people's approval, we will end up being disappointed time and time again. We can't allow people to mold us into what they want us to be. God uniquely equipped us with personalities and traits for the purpose that He put us on this earth to fulfill. So, we shouldn't feel bad if we're not like everybody else because God created us to be the way we are on purpose! "For you created my inmost being; you knit me together in my mother's womb. I praise you because I am fearfully and wonderfully made; your works are wonderful, I know that full well." Praise Him for who He is and for who we are in Him! Be Blessed!

Psalm 139:14

DAILY REFLECTIONS

AUGUST 3

Taming the Tongue

Do you pride yourself in always having to have the last word? Do you say things in anger that you later regret? Oftentimes, the best words our lips can speak are those that are left unspoken! "Those who guard their lips preserve their lives, but those who speak rashly will come to ruin." Be Blessed!

Proverbs 13:3

DAILY REFLECTIONS

___
___
___
___
___
___
___
___
___

AUGUST 4

Blessed to Serve

How many people know they are in a job they weren't qualified for? But somehow, they were able to move beyond more qualified candidates to secure the position. That is God's way of positioning them for the work He has destined for them to do. We all have a purpose to fulfill, and one of those is to bless others. So, don't question how you got the job, just know God will equip you for the work you are destined to do! "The Lord your God has blessed you in all the work of your hands." Be Blessed!

Deuteronomy 2:7

DAILY REFLECTIONS

AUGUST 5

Being a Good Steward Over Your Money

How good are you at managing your money? Are you responsible, or do you spend money frivolously? Do you give generously, or do you selfishly keep everything to yourself? God blesses you so that you can turn around and be a blessing to someone else. Therefore, you must be a good steward over your money so you will be able to bless someone else. "Each of you should use whatever gift you have received to serve others, as faithful stewards of God's grace in its various forms." As the Capital One commercial says, "What's in Your Wallet?" Be Blessed!

1 Peter 4:10

DAILY REFLECTIONS

_____
_____
_____
_____
_____
_____
_____
_____
_____

AUGUST 6

Blessings for Obedience

There are abundant blessings awaiting us when we choose to obey God. Foolishly, a lot people choose to follow their own paths. However, "all these blessings will come on you and accompany you if you obey the Lord your God":

- You will be blessed in the city and blessed in the country
- The fruit of your womb will be blessed
- The crops of your land will be blessed
- The young of your livestock will be blessed
- The calves of your herds and the lambs of your flocks will be blessed
- Your basket and your kneading trough will be blessed.
- You will be blessed when you come in and blessed when you go out.
- The land The Lord gives you will be blessed
- The Lord will make you the head and not the tail
- You will be a lender and not a borrower
- Everything you put your hand to will be blessed

Deuteronomy 28:2-14

DAILY REFLECTIONS

AUGUST 7

Authenticity

" God is a Spirit: and they that worship Him must worship Him in spirit and in truth." So, there is no point in trying to pretend to be something you're not, because God "created your inmost being" and He knows exactly who you are. Therefore, be true to yourself, and be true to your God! Be Blessed!

John 4:24, Psalm 139:13

DAILY REFLECTIONS

AUGUST 8

Spiritual Fatigue

Have you ever gotten so tired that you felt totally empty? You've poured into so many other people, but no one is pouring into you? As a result, you become fatigued and spiritually empty. What can you do to restore your joy? "Create in me a pure heart, O God, and renew a steadfast spirit within me. Do not cast me from your presence or take your Holy Spirit from me. Restore to me the joy of your salvation and grant me a willing spirit, to sustain me." Be Blessed!

Psalm 51:10-12

DAILY REFLECTIONS

AUGUST 9

Communication

Although communication is critical in every relationship, there are so many people who do not know how to effectively communicate with one another. Husbands and wives, parents and children, brothers and sisters, friends and co-workers, etc., don't know how to communicate with each other. Some of us even have a hard time communicating with God. But even when we don't know what to say to Him, He is always there ready to listen to us. "I sought the Lord, and He answered me; He delivered me from all my fears. Those who look to Him are radiant; their faces are never covered with shame. This poor man called, and the Lord heard him; He saved him out of all his troubles. The angel of the Lord encamps around those who fear Him, and He delivers them. Taste and see that the Lord is good; blessed is the man who takes refuge in Him." God, we thank you for your ever-present ear that attends to our cry! Be Blessed!

Psalm 34:4-8

DAILY REFLECTIONS

AUGUST 10

Anxiety

Have you ever been so anxious that it caused you to feel bad? "Anxiety weighs down the heart, but a kind word cheers it up." Therefore, if you ever find yourself in that state, surround yourself with people who will speak a kind word to you in order to build you back up! Be Blessed!

Proverbs 12:25

DAILY REFLECTIONS

_____
_____
_____
_____
_____
_____
_____
_____
_____
_____

AUGUST 11

Obedience

Your body is amazingly crafted. God gave your body the ability to signal you when you are hungry and to let you know when you're sleepy or tired. It even lets you know when you've had enough to eat by allowing you to feel full. However, many times you don't listen to the signals. You continue on with your busy life until you have to face the consequences of ignoring your body. Hopefully, at some point you will slow down and learn to take care of the body you have so graciously been given. If you don't, the alternative will not be pretty. "This day I call heaven and earth as witnesses against you that I have set before you life and death, blessings and curses. Now choose life, so that you and your children may live and that you may love the Lord your God, listen to his voice, and hold fast to him. For the Lord is your life, and he will give you many years in the land he swore to give to your fathers, Abraham, Isaac and Jacob." Be Blessed!

Deuteronomy 30:19-20

DAILY REFLECTIONS

AUGUST 12

Appearances Can Be Deceiving

So often we get caught up in outward appearances and what people look like. That's why it's so easy for people to be fooled by "the representative." When you base your opinions and/or feelings about a person solely on their physical appearance, you become vulnerable to pretense and deceit. Looks can be deceiving, and beauty is only skin deep. Therefore, don't judge a book by its cover! "But the Lord said to Samuel, "Do not consider his appearance or his height, for I have rejected him. The Lord does not look at the things people look at. People look at the outward appearance, but the Lord looks at the heart." Be Blessed!

1 Samuel 16:7

DAILY REFLECTIONS

_____
_____
_____
_____
_____
_____
_____
_____

AUGUST 13

Praying in Faith

When you pray in faith believing what you have prayed for will come to pass, you can start praising God now, instead of waiting until it happens. "Now faith is confidence in what we hope for and assurance about what we do not see." Be Blessed!

Hebrews 11:1

DAILY REFLECTIONS
___
___
___
___
___
___
___
___
___

AUGUST 14

Meditation

What are you focusing your thoughts on? Do you meditate on the Word of God? It is important to feed your spirit with the Word of God, to help you in times of trouble. "If your law had not been my delight, I would have perished in my affliction. I will never forget your precepts, for by them you have preserved my life." Be Blessed!

Psalm 119:92-93

DAILY REFLECTIONS

AUGUST 15

Righteousness

How do you react when adversity comes your way? If there was a hidden camera around to tape your behavior, would it be something you would be proud of or embarrassed by? Because God is omnipresent, He sees everything you do even when no one else does. So, in essence, God *is* your hidden camera! Therefore, you want to live your life in a way that would make God proud. "Be very careful, then, how you live—not as unwise but as wise, making the most of every opportunity." Be Blessed!

Ephesians 5:15-16

DAILY REFLECTIONS

AUGUST 16

Possibilities of God

There are so many situations we face on a daily basis that cause us to feel hopeless with no way out. However, whether we face terminal illness, financial disparity, emotional despair, etc., God is greater than them all. "With man this is impossible, but with God all things are possible." Be Blessed!

Matthew 19:26

DAILY REFLECTIONS

_____
_____
_____
_____
_____
_____
_____
_____
_____
_____

AUGUST 17

His Marvelous Deeds

There have been times when we have been in situations where it appeared there was no way out. However, God stepped in and miraculously worked it out. In situations like that all we can do is give Him the praise He is due. "Praise be to the Lord God, the God of Israel, who alone does marvelous deeds." Be Blessed!

Psalm 72:18

DAILY REFLECTIONS

AUGUST 18

Seasons

We're in a time where we can no longer take life for granted. There is a time and a season for everything that happens in our life. So, we should live our lives in faith; striving to be all that we can be for the time that we are privileged to be here. "There is a time for everything, and a season for every activity under heaven. A time to live and a time to die." Be Blessed!

Ecclesiastes 3:1

DAILY REFLECTIONS

AUGUST 19

Persistence

Sometimes it feels like we're just spinning wheels and never getting anywhere. However, if we can just hang in there a little while, God will attend to our every need. "Therefore we do not lose heart. Though outwardly we are wasting away, yet inwardly we are being renewed day by day." Be Blessed!

2 Corinthians 4:16

DAILY REFLECTIONS

AUGUST 20

Intercession

Lord, we continue to solicit Your divine intervention regarding the disasters around the world. Please stop the senseless madness that is going on over here and overseas. We know You created us for more than this. So, we are praying on behalf of those who are in need right now. Please keep us under Your hedge of protection and lead us in the way we should go. Speak peace to our storms and everlasting joy in our lives. You are an awesome God, and we bask in Your glory. We give You all the honor and all the praise. Thank You for being a faithful and loving God! "I urge, then, first of all, that petitions, prayers, intercession and thanksgiving be made for all people." Be Blessed!

1 Timothy 2:1

DAILY REFLECTIONS

AUGUST 21

Trust

We put our trust in a lot people who don't deserve it. However, "Blessed is the one who trusts in the Lord, whose confidence is in Him." When you put your faith and trust in God, you won't need anybody else! Be Blessed!

Jeremiah 17:7

DAILY REFLECTIONS

AUGUST 22

Deliverance

What do you do when life throws you a curve ball? You catch it and you throw it back! There will be situations in your life that will rock you to the core. The doctor may give you a bad report, you may lose your job, your relationship may fall apart, etc. However, your reaction to the circumstance will determine how it plays out. Trials will come, but they don't have to take you out. You serve a God who will answer when you call! "The Lord is my rock, my fortress and my deliverer; my God is my rock, in whom I take refuge. He is my shield and the horn of my salvation, my stronghold. I call to the Lord, who is worthy of praise, and I am saved from my enemies." So, call out to Him when you are in distress, and He *will* attend to your need! Be Blessed!

Psalm 18:2-3

DAILY REFLECTIONS

_____
_____
_____
_____
_____
_____
_____
_____
_____

AUGUST 23

Relationship with God

Washing our face, combing our hair, taking a bath and getting dressed are things that we do every day without even thinking about it. We should also be spending quality time with God every day, but we don't want it to become something we do without thinking about it. God desires an intimate, up close personal relationship with us, and He wants the same thing in return from us. So, just as we express our love to each other, we can let God know how we feel about Him! "As the deer pants for streams of water, so my soul pants for you, O God." Be Blessed!

Psalm 42:1

DAILY REFLECTIONS

AUGUST 24

Humility

When someone gives you a compliment, how do you respond? Are you comfortable with it, or do you brush it off and respond with a negative statement like, "this old thing?" So many people are used to being put down or criticized that when someone gives them a compliment they don't know how to accept it. Here's a thought, just say "thank you"—nothing more, nothing less! Simply saying "thank you" acknowledges your appreciation of the compliment, but also eliminates the temptation of becoming vain or conceited. "God opposes the proud but gives grace to the humble." So, learn to be grateful for the compliment without letting it go to your head. Be Blessed!

James 4:6

DAILY REFLECTIONS

AUGUST 25

Destiny

You spend the majority of your day at work, so you might as well enjoy it! If you are in a job you dread going to every day, then you need to think long and hard about staying there. What is keeping you from attaining your "dream job?" Is it fear of the unknown? Is it a lack of opportunity? Is it complacency? Whatever it is, you must move past it! You have been blessed with many gifts and talents and you don't want to waste them by staying on a job where you are not being fruitful. So, pray about it and ask God for direction. He will never steer you wrong! "The Lord will guide you always; He will satisfy your needs in a sun-scorched land and will strengthen your frame. You will be like a well-watered garden, like a spring whose waters never fail." Therefore, seek His guidance, and then get ready to move. Be Blessed!

Isaiah 48:11

DAILY REFLECTIONS

_____
_____
_____
_____
_____
_____
_____
_____

AUGUST 26

Forgiveness

Have you ever been angry with someone in the past but refused to forgive them? Your relationship with them will never be right until you forgive them and move past it. The same goes with your relationship with God. There may have been times in your life when you have been angry with God for allowing certain things to happen in your life. Because you have not gotten over it and forgiven God, you are still harboring anger and resentment and it is affecting your relationship with Him. So, now when you call on Him, you feel as if He is not there or answering your prayers. However, God has not forgotten you. He is still there, but you must let go of the hurt and pain and get back in right relationship with Him. If God can forgive you for all the things you have done in your life, then surely you can forgive Him! "Therefore I tell you, whatever you ask for in prayer, believe that you have received it, and it will be yours. And when you stand praying, if you hold anything against anyone, forgive him, so that your Father in heaven may forgive you your sins." Be Blessed!

Mark 11:24-25

DAILY REFLECTIONS

AUGUST 27

Victory

We all have crosses to bear. For some it may be an unhealthy relationship, for another it may be an unhealthy habit or addiction, and still for others it may be an unhealthy lifestyle, etc. However, we don't have to stay stuck in these situations. God has made us "more than conquerors," so we can be victorious in our relationships, our habits, and our health. Be Blessed!

Romans 8:37

DAILY REFLECTIONS

AUGUST 28

Determination

Have you ever wanted desperately to change a behavior but felt powerless to do anything about it? The enemy would have you believe that what you are trying to achieve is impossible. However, you must remember "everything is possible for him who believes." So, no matter how hard it seems, just know you can do it! "I can do all things through Christ who strengthens me." Be Blessed!

Mark 9:23, Philippians 4:13

DAILY REFLECTIONS

AUGUST 29

Assurance

We are often suspicious of things that sound too good to be true. That's because we've been taught "if it sounds too good to be true, it usually is." But we can't think that way about God, because His Word is true, and His love is unconditional. He may sound too good to be true, but we can rest assured that "God is not a man that He should lie" and He will do just what He said! "Praise be to the Lord, who has given rest to His people Israel just as He promised. Not one word has failed of all the good promises He gave through His servant Moses." Be Blessed!

Number 23:19, 1 Kings 8:56

DAILY REFLECTIONS

AUGUST 30

Worry

You will experience true freedom when you no longer have to worry about the cares and concerns of life. Although you may encounter circumstances, they don't have to stress you out or cause you anxiety. "Who of you by worrying can add a single hour to his life? "And why do you worry about clothes? See how the lilies of the field grow. They do not labor or spin. Yet I tell you that not even Solomon in all his splendor was dressed like one of these. If that is how God clothes the grass of the field, which is here today and tomorrow is thrown into the fire, will He not much more clothe you, O you of little faith? So do not worry, saying, 'What shall we eat?' or 'What shall we drink?' or 'What shall we wear?' For the pagans run after all these things, and your heavenly Father knows that you need them." Therefore, since you are a child of the King and He owns "the cattle on a thousand hills," you don't have to worry or be anxious because you can trust that He will take care of you! Be Blessed!

Matthew 6:27-32, Psalm 50:10

DAILY REFLECTIONS

AUGUST 31

Faith

There will be times in your life when you are faced with situations that take you out of your comfort zone; situations that require you to think outside the box. So, when that time comes, what should you do? Seek God's guidance first, and then be willing to step out on faith. It may unnerve you a little at first, but the only way to get over fear is to confront it. "The Lord is my light and my salvation—whom shall I fear? The Lord is the stronghold of my life—of whom shall I be afraid? When evil men advance against me to devour my flesh, when my enemies and my foes attack me, they will stumble and fall. Though an army besiege me, my heart will not fear; though war break out against me, even then will I be confident." So, as a result of that confidence, you can step outside your comfort zone and do something different! You no longer have to be afraid to think outside the box! Be Blessed!

Psalm 27:1-3

DAILY REFLECTIONS

_____
_____
_____
_____
_____
_____
_____
_____
_____

SEPTEMBER 1

Fellowship

It is so easy for us to fall into a "withdrawal mode." We get in a rut and lose interest in the things we used to love to do. We sometimes even lose interest in fellowshipping with others. We stay to ourselves and withdraw from the world. However, this is the devil's way of trying to get us alone so he can distort our thinking. He isolates us so he can fill our minds with wrong thinking, then he can eventually lead us to wrongdoing! But we can't let him do that because "all wrongdoing is sin." So, even though we may not feel like praying, going to church, or even fellowshipping with others, we must do it anyway so that we "do not give the devil a foothold." Prayer renews our spirit and keeps us in close relationship with God. Going to church and hearing God's Word is the spiritual renewal that keeps us energized throughout the week; and fellowshipping with others is a mandate from God. "If we claim to have fellowship with Him yet walk in the darkness, we lie and do not live by the truth. But if we walk in the light, as He is in the light, we have fellowship with one another, and the blood of Jesus, His Son, purifies us from all sin." Be Blessed!

1 John 1:6-7, 5:17, Ephesians 4:27

DAILY REFLECTIONS

SEPTEMBER 2

Complacency

When we find ourselves stuck in a rut, we can't just wallow in it. We've got to move! It may be easier to keep things the "status quo," but that's not the best thing for us. We were created with a purpose in mind so it's time for us to get out there and do it! "In Him we were also chosen, having been predestined according to the plan of Him who works out everything in conformity with the purpose of His will, in order that we, who were the first to hope in Christ, might be for the praise of His glory." Be Blessed!

Ephesians 1:11-12

DAILY REFLECTIONS
_____
_____
_____
_____
_____
_____
_____
_____
_____
_____

SEPTEMBER 3

Forgiveness

Do you have a problem forgiving people? Do you find it hard to forgive and forget? It's easy to forgive someone when they've done something insignificant. But how successful are you at forgiving people when they've done something hurtful or harmful? Most people have a hard time doing it; however, that is what you are supposed to do as a Christian. The reason it's so difficult is because you're trying to do it in your own strength. You need the Lord's assistance to deal with the big stuff like lying, stealing, cheating, etc.! Those kinds of breaches of trust take real soul searching and a commitment to change. Therefore, you will need God's saving grace, because if you can't forgive and forget, you won't be able to move on with your life. You'll continue to hold on to it and keep bringing up the hurt over and over again. So, solicit God's help in your struggle. He has plenty of experience and patience from having to forgive you! "Be merciful, just as your Father is merciful. "Do not judge, and you will not be judged. Do not condemn, and you will not be condemned. Forgive, and you will be forgiven." Be Blessed!

Luke 6:36-37

DAILY REFLECTIONS

SEPTEMBER 4

Sin

Hypertension is referred to as the "silent killer." It is called the silent killer because so many people suffer from it but don't even know it. So many times sin can become a "silent killer" as well. The more we sin, the easier it becomes. We may experience guilt at first, but eventually our hearts become hardened to it and we do it without even thinking about it. That is how it silently kills us. Since "the wages of sin is death," every time we sin we kill ourselves slowly. But it doesn't have to be that way! Jesus "was delivered over to death for our sins and was raised to life for our justification." "Now that you have been set free from sin and have become slaves to God, the benefit you reap leads to holiness, and the result is eternal life. For the wages of sin is death, but the gift of God is eternal life in Christ Jesus our Lord." Be Blessed!

Romans 4:25, 6:22-23

DAILY REFLECTIONS

SEPTEMBER 5

Omniscience

Isn't it a wonderful thing to be able to serve a God who knows your every thought and who will attend to your every need? "O Lord, you have searched me, and you know me. You know when I sit and when I rise; you perceive my thoughts from afar. You discern my going out and my lying down; you are familiar with all my ways. Before a word is on my tongue you know it completely, O Lord." "God will meet all your needs according to His glorious riches in Christ Jesus. To our God and Father be glory for ever and ever. Amen." Be Blessed!

Psalm 139:1-4, Philippians 4:19-20

DAILY REFLECTIONS

SEPTEMBER 6

Trust

Sometimes we face difficult situations in life and we don't know which way to turn. We have so many decisions to make that it can be overwhelming. The best thing to do is to stop stressing out and "be still." If we get quiet enough, we may just hear what God is trying to tell us! "The Lord Almighty is with us; the God of Jacob is our fortress. Selah. Come and see the works of the Lord, the desolations He has brought on the earth. He makes wars cease to the ends of the earth; He breaks the bow and shatters the spear, He burns the shields with fire. "Be still, and know that I am God; I will be exalted among the nations, I will be exalted in the earth." Be Blessed!

Psalm 46:7-10

DAILY REFLECTIONS

SEPTEMBER 7

Provision

Even in a bleak economy, you can still have joy. You serve a God who can provide even in a famine. So, as hard as it may be to keep the faith, you have no other choice. God did not bring you this far to leave you now. Therefore, you can trust Him to keep His promise to you as you follow and keep His commands. "The Lord will grant you abundant prosperity—in the fruit of your womb, the young of your livestock and the crops of your ground—in the land He swore to your forefathers to give you. The Lord will open the heavens, the storehouse of His bounty, to send rain on your land in season and to bless all the work of your hands. You will lend to many nations but will borrow from none. The Lord will make you the head, not the tail. If you pay attention to the commands of the Lord your God that I give you this day and carefully follow them, you will always be at the top, never at the bottom." Hallelujah!

Deuteronomy 28:11-13

DAILY REFLECTIONS

SEPTEMBER 8

Standing on the Promises of His Word

There will be times when you will have to exercise your faith even in the most difficult times. The doctor may give you a bad report, or you can't seem to make ends meet, or even when you can't see a way out. Those are the times when you will need to stand on God's promises and believe in what His Word says. Meditate on scriptures like, "I am the God that healeth thee," or "God shall supply all of your needs according to His riches in Christ Jesus," or even "The name of the Lord is a strong tower; the righteous run to it and are safe." You can trust God to see you through. "The statutes of the Lord are trustworthy." Be Blessed!

Exodus 15:26, Philippians 4:19, Proverbs 18:10, Psalm 19:7

DAILY REFLECTIONS

___
___
___
___
___
___
___
___
___
___

SEPTEMBER 9

Refuge

❝ O Taste and see that the Lord is good; blessed is the man who takes refuge in Him." We often spend needless time worrying about what is yet to come. However, if we remember the safety we have in God, we can rest in His assurance. He promises to keep us and never leave us. Therefore, we can take comfort in the refuge He so freely gives to us. Be Blessed!

Psalm 34:8

DAILY REFLECTIONS

_____
_____
_____
_____
_____
_____
_____
_____
_____
_____

SEPTEMBER 10

Procrastination

We often make excuses for things we don't want to do. We can rationalize our way out of anything if we try hard enough. However, the bottom line is, excuses don't get things done, actions do! Therefore, instead of coming up with reasons why we can't do something, we need to concentrate on figuring out how we can! "Everything is possible for him who believes." Be Blessed!

Mark 9:23

DAILY REFLECTIONS

SEPTEMBER 11

Discipline

What makes us continue to do things we know are wrong? Things like, continuing to eat the wrong foods when we know we need to lose weight, or continuing a relationship that we know we shouldn't be in, or continuing to participate in an addiction that we know will eventually kill us? We keep doing it because we rationalize our behavior. We make excuses why we can't lose weight rather than admit we're not being as disciplined as we could be. We lie to ourselves about our relationships so we won't feel bad about staying in a bad, abusive, or sometimes even adulterous relationship. And we even lie to ourselves about our addictions saying, "Well, I have to die from something." However, that's not God's best for us. He wants us to experience the fullness of His joy, free from sin and destruction. So, let us accept the redemption He has given us and turn from those ways that are not pleasing to Him! "For He has rescued us from the dominion of darkness and brought us into the kingdom of the Son He loves, in whom we have redemption, the forgiveness of sins." Be Blessed!

Colossians 1:13-14

DAILY REFLECTIONS

SEPTEMBER 12

Gratefulness

Have you ever heard someone say, "The Lord has blessed me to wake up this morning in my right mind?" So often people take that reality for granted! However, since people lose their mind every day to diseases like dementia, that's not a reality we can afford to take for granted. So thank God every day for keeping *you* in your right mind! "Those who live according to the sinful nature have their minds set on what that nature desires; but those who live in accordance with the Spirit have their minds set on what the Spirit desires. The mind of a sinful man is death, but the mind controlled by the Spirit is life and peace." Be Blessed!

Romans 8:5-6

DAILY REFLECTIONS

SEPTEMBER 13

Step Out in Faith

We get so used to the status quo that we forget to use our creativity and vision. Sometimes we need to think about, look at, and do things differently. "If we always do what we've always done, then we'll continue to get what we've always gotten." When God called Abraham to go forth, Abraham didn't know where he was going, but he trusted God enough to step out and go anyway. "By faith Abraham, when called to go to a place he would later receive as his inheritance, obeyed and went, even though he did not know where he was going." We need to have the same blind faith to trust God, even when we don't know where He's leading us. Be Blessed!

Hebrews 11:8

DAILY REFLECTIONS

SEPTEMBER 14

Stress

Have you ever noticed how carefree and laidback animals and children are? They bounce around without a care in the world! The reason they can do that is because they don't worry. They don't have to worry about food, shelter, clothing, bills, bosses, health, or any of those things. But guess what? Neither do you! You may have challenges in your life, but you don't have to stress over them. Children have challenges, too, but they trust their parents to take care of them. That's the same thing you need to do! You have a heavenly Father who sits high and looks low, and He's standing by ready to take care of your every need. "So do not worry, saying, 'What shall we eat?' or 'What shall we drink?' or 'What shall we wear?' For the pagans run after all these things, and your heavenly Father knows that you need them. But seek first His kingdom and His righteousness, and all these things will be given to you as well." Be Blessed!

Matthew 6:31-33

DAILY REFLECTIONS

SEPTEMBER 15

Health

Oftentimes we take for granted the simple pleasure of having activity of our limbs and a reasonable portion of health and strength. But on those days when we don't move as fast as we normally do, or the "snap, crackle, and pop" we hear in the morning isn't coming from our Rice Krispies cereal, then we gain a little more appreciation for the blessing of good health. "I pray that you may enjoy good health and that all may go well with you, even as your soul is getting along well." Be Blessed!

3 John 1:2

DAILY REFLECTIONS

SEPTEMBER 16

Change

If there are situations in your life you don't like, with God's help, you have the power to change them. You may not be able to do anything on your own; however, with God's omniscience, omnipresence, and omnipotence, you can do all things! "I can do all things through Christ who strengthens me." Believe that and be blessed!

Philippians 4:13

DAILY REFLECTIONS

SEPTEMBER 17

Self Care

Your body lets you know when you're tired, hungry, thirsty, satisfied, etc. The problem is you don't listen to the signals! You keep eating, even though you know you are full. You stay up late, even though you know you are tired. Some people even ignore the signals their body gives them when they need to eliminate waste; which later on causes unnecessary constipation. So, why do you do this? Because you stay too busy and forget to take care of yourself! You only have one body, so you need to start making it a priority. "Don't you know that you yourselves are God's temple and that God's Spirit lives in you? If anyone destroys God's temple, God will destroy him; for God's temple is sacred, and you are that temple." So, starting today; be good to God's temple and start taking care of *you*. Be Blessed!

1 Corinthians 3:16-17

DAILY REFLECTIONS

SEPTEMBER 18

Resistance

When the unexpected happens in our lives, how do we react? Do we resist it, or do we accept it with a good attitude? If we resist something that God allows, it's saying we question His ability to see us through. It may be unexpected to us, but it's no surprise to God! Our steps are ordered by Him and He's already worked it all out. Therefore, we can embrace anything that God does, because we can trust that He knows what He's doing. "The Lord has done this, and it is marvelous in our eyes. This is the day the Lord has made; let us rejoice and be glad in it." Be Blessed!

Psalm 118:23-24

DAILY REFLECTIONS
_____
_____
_____
_____
_____
_____
_____
_____
_____

SEPTEMBER 19

Steadfastness

When things looked like they were over for Jesus, He surprised everyone when He rose from the dead on the third day. It looked like it was over, but in the end, He reigned! So, when you are tempted to get discouraged and feel like you can't go on, remember it isn't over until God says it's over! "Where, O death, is your victory? Where, O death, is your sting?" The sting of death is sin, and the power of sin is the law. But thanks be to God! He gives us the victory through our Lord Jesus Christ. Therefore, my dear brothers, stand firm. Let nothing move you. Always give yourselves fully to the work of the Lord, because you know that your labor in the Lord is not in vain." Be Blessed!

1 Corinthians 15:55-58

DAILY REFLECTIONS

SEPTEMBER 20

Self-Control

Most people have something they like to do that could get out of control if they didn't use discipline. Thankfully, God knows that, and He provides a way of escape. "No temptation has seized you except what is common to man. And God is faithful; He will not let you be tempted beyond what you can bear. But when you are tempted, He will also provide a way out so that you can stand up under it." You must be willing, however, to exercise discipline and self-control. People fail at overcoming indulgence because they expect God to do it all. Even though He provides a way of escape, you have to be willing to take it! "Therefore, prepare your minds for action; be self-controlled; set your hope fully on the grace to be given you when Jesus Christ is revealed. As obedient children do not conform to the evil desires you had when you lived in ignorance. But just as He who called you is holy, so be holy in all you do." Be Blessed!

1 Corinthians 10:13, 1 Peter 1:13-15

DAILY REFLECTIONS

SEPTEMBER 21

God's Report

Oftentimes, we are so quick to believe what other people tell us about our destiny that we fail to listen to what God says. His report is the only one we should believe! "Do not believe every spirit, but test the spirits to see whether they are from God, because many false prophets have gone out into the world." Whose report shall we believe? We shall believe the report of The Lord! Be Blessed!

John 4:1

DAILY REFLECTIONS

SEPTEMBER 22

Make God a Priority in Your Life

Are you giving God your all? Do you put God first in your life? Although you have other obligations in your life, nothing should come before your relationship with God. God desires to have an up close, personal, and intimate relationship with you. He doesn't need any puffed up, insincere praise. He wants the real you! So, make God a priority in your life and watch Him speak peace to your storms! "May the God of hope fill you with all joy and peace as you trust in Him, so that you may overflow with hope by the power of the Holy Spirit." Be Blessed!

Romans 15:13

DAILY REFLECTIONS

SEPTEMBER 23

Positivity

Have you ever been guilty of talking negatively about something and then have it end up becoming a reality? That's because you've spoken it into being and made it a self-fulfilling prophesy. However, if you can speak negatively and will something to happen, why not speak positively about your situations so you will have a positive outcome? "Out of the same mouth come praise and cursing. My brothers, this should not be." Therefore, make a conscious decision to start letting only positive things come out of your mouth! So, "do not let any unwholesome talk come out of your mouths." Be Blessed!

James 3:10, Ephesians 4:29

DAILY REFLECTIONS

SEPTEMBER 24

Healing

God's healing power knows no boundaries. We may put limitations on God; however, His powers are limitless. The doctor may give you a bad report, but God can turn their diagnosis completely around! "I will exalt you, O Lord, for you lifted me out of the depths and did not let my enemies gloat over me. O Lord my God, I called to you for help and you healed me." Thank you for being a God that heals! Be Blessed!

Psalm 30:1-2

DAILY REFLECTIONS

SEPTEMBER 25

Stress

During these times when people are stressed out and under pressure, you must remember prayer is a great stress reliever! "And pray in the Spirit on all occasions with all kinds of prayers and requests." "Do not be anxious about anything, but in everything, by prayer and petition, with Thankfulness, present your requests to God. And the peace of God, which transcends all understanding, will guard your hearts and your minds in Christ Jesus." Remember, you are too blessed to be stressed! Be Blessed!

Ephesians 6:18, Philippians 4:6-7

DAILY REFLECTIONS

_____
_____
_____
_____
_____
_____
_____
_____
_____

SEPTEMBER 26

Goodwill Towards Others

All 50 states have "Good Samaritan" laws that legally protect people who willingly give emergency care to ill or injured persons without accepting anything in return. The law was patterned after a Samaritan in the Bible who helped a stranger who had been beaten and robbed and left for dead. Two others had passed the man on the road but chose to pass him by. However, the Samaritan stopped to take care of him and took him to a safe place where he could get well. We, too, should follow his example and be kind to one another without expecting anything in return. "A man was going down from Jerusalem to Jericho, when he fell into the hands of robbers. They stripped him of his clothes, beat him and went away, leaving him half dead. A priest happened to be going down the same road, and when he saw the man, he passed by on the other side. So too, a Levite, when he came to the place and saw him, passed by on the other side. But a Samaritan, as he traveled, came where the man was; and when he saw him, he took pity on him. He went to him and bandaged his wounds, pouring on oil and wine. Then he put the man on his own donkey, took him to an inn and took care of him." Let us remember to always look out for our fellow-man and "go and do likewise" as Jesus advises us to do! Be Blessed!

Luke 10:30-34, 37

DAILY REFLECTIONS

SEPTEMBER 27

Fearful and Wonderful

I received an e-mail one day asking for an explanation of the term "fearfully and wonderfully made." My understanding is that God created us in such a way that people should be in awe of us and reverence us. In Job 1:1, Job was described as a man that was blameless and upright because he "feared God and shunned evil." In this reference the point is being made that because Job loved and reverenced God so much, he wouldn't even think about doing evil. This use of the word fearful does not have anything to do with being afraid. Instead it is just the opposite. To be fearfully and wonderfully made means that God has made you so awesome that you are to be greatly admired. So, step up to the plate and be that fearful and wonderful man or woman that God created you to be. Be Blessed!

Psalm 139:14, Job 1:1

DAILY REFLECTIONS

SEPTEMBER 28

Fear

So many times we worry and have doubts about the plans God has for our lives. Some of us are even afraid to step out and do what we know God has called us to do! But if God has called us to do it, then He will equip us with the necessary skills to achieve it. "For I know the plans I have for you," declares the Lord, "plans to prosper you and not to harm you, plans to give you hope and a future." So, we can rest in His assurance to fulfill His promise over our lives. We don't have to be afraid, because "God did not give us a spirit of fear." We don't have to worry, because we are not to "be anxious about anything." We don't have to stay in bondage because, "Who the Son sets free is free indeed." Be Blessed!

Jeremiah 29:11, 2 Timothy 1:7, Philippians 4:6, John 8:36

DAILY REFLECTIONS

SEPTEMBER 29

Spiritual Warfare

When the enemy comes to attack us with his lies, you must strike them down with the truth of God's Word. In order to do that, you must first know God's Word. Attending a structured Bible Study will help you gain knowledge in that area. So the next time the devil comes with his foolishness and lies, be armed and ready with the sword of God's Word! "Therefore put on the full armor of God, so that when the day of evil comes, you may be able to stand your ground, and after you have done everything, to stand. Stand firm then, with the belt of truth buckled around your waist, with the breastplate of righteousness in place, and with your feet fitted with the readiness that comes from the gospel of peace. In addition to all this, take up the shield of faith, with which you can extinguish all the flaming arrows of the evil one. Take the helmet of salvation and the sword of the Spirit, which is the word of God." Be Blessed!

Ephesians 6:13-17

DAILY REFLECTIONS

SEPTEMBER 30

Everlasting Love

"You, God, are my God, earnestly I seek you; I thirst for you, my whole being longs for you, in a dry and parched land where there is no water." How wonderful it is to have a love like that! Be Blessed!

Psalm 63:1

DAILY REFLECTIONS

OCTOBER 1

Purpose

What have you accomplished this year thus far? Most people's New Year's Resolutions have long been forgotten. However, I hope you are walking in victory and purpose! So often people glide through life without ever giving thought to why they are even here. God created each of us with a purpose and destiny and it's up to us to fulfill it. If you're unsure what your purpose in life is, ask God, then stand still until His will is clear! "If any man seeks wisdom, let Him ask of God. You have not because you ask not and when you ask you ask amiss."

James 1:5

DAILY REFLECTIONS

OCTOBER 2

Love

We are so blessed to have a loving God, who loves us unconditionally. "But you, O Lord, are a compassionate and gracious God, slow to anger, abounding in love and faithfulness." A lot of us don't even love ourselves that way! But God charges us to "love our neighbor as we love ourselves." Therefore, we need to start learning how to love ourselves (flaws and all), so we can be open and free to love others! "Love is patient, love is kind. It does not envy, it does not boast, it is not proud. It is not rude, it is not self-seeking, it is not easily angered, it keeps no record of wrong. Love does not delight in evil, but rejoices in the truth. It always protects, always trusts, always hopes, always perseveres. Love never fails." So, open up your heart and learn how to love yourself and others! Be Blessed!

Psalm 86:15, Matthew 19:19, 1 Corinthians 13:4-8

DAILY REFLECTIONS

OCTOBER 3

In His Presence

David said in Psalm 34, "I will bless the Lord at all times: His praise shall continually be in my mouth." Further down in verse 8 he says, "O taste and see that the Lord is good: blessed is the man that trusts in Him." If you've ever experienced the Lord's presence for yourself, you know there is nothing else like it! No amount of alcohol, drug, sex, food, etc. can come close to the feeling of God's loving arms around you. Some people spend their whole life chasing after temporary fixes they think will fill the void in their lives. But I'm here to tell you, the only thing that can fill the empty places in your life is an up close, personal relationship with God. He is the only thing that can complete you! Once you realize that, you can stop chasing after meaningless things. "Seek your happiness in God, and He will give you the desires of your heart." Be Blessed!

Psalm 34:1-8, 37:4

DAILY REFLECTIONS

_____
_____
_____
_____
_____
_____
_____
_____
_____
_____

OCTOBER 4

The Promises of God

When you go through difficult financial circumstances, hold on to the promise that "my God shall supply all of my needs according to His riches in Christ Jesus." Remember, the same God that made a way before will make a way now. "He owns the cattle on a thousand hills" and as His children, we have access to it! So, don't get discouraged and stressed out trying to figure out how you're going to make it, just know that He will come through right on time! Be Blessed!

Philippians 4:19, Psalm 50:10,

DAILY REFLECTIONS

OCTOBER 5

The Enemy's Attacks

Even when we feel we're being attacked on every side, we must remember what Paul said in 2 Corinthians 4:8-9, "We are hard pressed on every side, yet not crushed, perplexed but not in despair, persecuted, but not forsaken, struck down, but not destroyed." Believe that and Be Blessed!

2 Corinthians 4:8-9

DAILY REFLECTIONS

OCTOBER 6

Building Others Up

" Do not let any unwholesome talk come out of your mouths, but only what is helpful for building others up according to their needs, that it may benefit those who listen." Therefore, before you utter a word, ask yourself if your words will build up the person you're talking to. If the answer is no, then keep those words to yourself. Be Blessed!

Ephesians 4:29

DAILY REFLECTIONS

OCTOBER 7

Trust

When we struggle with something in our lives, do we take it to God in prayer? If so, we can rest assured that God has heard our prayer, and He will answer our cry. It may not be in the manner in which we want to receive it, but God *will* answer. Sometimes God says "no," sometimes He says, "yes," but sometimes God says, "not yet." Just as we would not want to have a premature baby, we don't want to birth our destiny before it is time either! God is never late, but He is never early either. He is always right on time! "Let us not become weary in doing good, for at the proper time we will reap a harvest if we do not give up." Be Blessed!

Galatians 6:9

DAILY REFLECTIONS

OCTOBER 8

Never Alone

In our lifetime, people will come and go. Some leave voluntarily, some pass away. However, God promised never to leave us alone. "Be content with what you have, because God has said, "Never will I leave you; never will I forsake you." Be Blessed!

Hebrews 13:5

DAILY REFLECTIONS

___
___
___
___
___
___
___
___
___

OCTOBER 9

Motives

Most of us, if given a little time, can eventually forgive someone for wronging us. What we struggle with is putting it behind us so we don't hold it against them forever! Our prayer should be to follow God's example as He forgives us. "The LORD is compassionate and gracious, slow to anger, abounding in love. He will not always accuse, nor will He harbor His anger forever; He does not treat us as our sins deserve or repay us according to our iniquities. For as high as the heavens are above the earth, so great is His love for those who fear Him; as far as the east is from the west, so far has He removed our transgressions from us. As a father has compassion on his children, so the LORD has compassion on those who fear Him; for He knows how we are formed, He remembers that we are dust." Let us exercise that same kind of compassion with one another! Be Blessed!!

Proverbs 16:2, 1 Corinthians 4:5

DAILY REFLECTIONS

OCTOBER 10

Faith

What a great time to be alive! Too often we focus on the circumstances in our immediate view and become discouraged. But I encourage you to focus on the awesome deliverance that is yet to come! If you are a believer, then your faith should remind you that whatever you are going through right now is only temporary. Continue to stand on your faith knowing that God is going to bring you out. When you act on your faith by praying without ceasing and continuing to believe no matter what, you are proving that you're not just talking the talk but are walking the walk! Remember, "Faith without works is dead." Be Blessed!

James 2:17

DAILY REFLECTIONS

_____
_____
_____
_____
_____
_____
_____
_____

OCTOBER 11

Assurance

Some people believe if you expect the worst, then you'll never be disappointed if things don't work out. The problem with that theory, however, is that you get what you expect! Therefore, you will continually create situations that turn out to be self-fulfilling prophesies. For example, you get involved in relationships with people who are emotionally or physically unavailable, so you won't have to take the risk of opening up your heart to them. However, if you never take any risks, you never accomplish anything. You must focus your attention on the one who is able to see you through any trial or tribulation. Such as with Peter, as long as he kept his eyes on Jesus, he was able to walk on the water. It is only when he took his eyes off Jesus and began worrying about the storm that he began to sink. You can rest assured that if you keep your eyes on Jesus, you won't have to live your life expecting the worst because even when the enemy plans to do evil, God will work it out for your good! Be Blessed!

Matthew 14:25-33

DAILY REFLECTIONS

OCTOBER 12

Continuous Praise

Have you ever praised God in the midst of a storm? When you know who calms the storm, you can praise Him even while you're still in it. "I will bless the Lord at all times, His praise shall continually be in my mouth!" Be Blessed!

Psalm 34:1

DAILY REFLECTIONS

_____
_____
_____
_____
_____
_____
_____
_____
_____

OCTOBER 13

Generational Blessings

So often, people believe their actions only matter for the present moment. However, the things we do today not only affect us, but also on generations to come. So, if we want our families to continue to be blessed, we must follow God's Word and be obedient to His Will. "From everlasting to everlasting the Lord's love is with those who fear Him, and His righteousness with their children's children—with those who keep His covenant and remember to obey His precepts." Be Blessed!

Psalm 103:17-18

DAILY REFLECTIONS

OCTOBER 14

Provision

God's word is true, even in a famine. The state of the economy may have everyone a little nervous and anxious about their finances right now, but God is still able to provide even in a famine! "The eyes of the Lord are on those who fear Him, on those whose hope is in His unfailing love, to deliver them from death and keep them alive in famine. We wait in hope for the Lord; He is our help and our shield. In Him our hearts rejoice, for we trust in His holy name. May your unfailing love rest upon us, O Lord, even as we put our hope in you." Be Blessed!

Psalm 33:18-22

DAILY REFLECTIONS

OCTOBER 15

Salvation

Just as there are two sides to every story, there are also two ways to look at a situation. However, when it comes to God, there is only one way! "I am the way and the truth and the life. No one comes to the Father except through me." You can't get any plainer than that. Enough said! Be Blessed!

John 14:6

DAILY REFLECTIONS

_____
_____
_____
_____
_____
_____
_____
_____
_____
_____

OCTOBER 16

Positivity

When we speak life to our situations, we see changes for the better. However, if we speak negatively about them, then a negative outcome is what we'll get. Because "death and life are in the power of the tongue" we have to be very careful of what we say! "Have faith in God," Jesus answered. "I tell you the truth, if anyone says to this mountain, 'Go, throw yourself into the sea,' and does not doubt in his heart but believes that what he says will happen, it will be done for him." So, remember, speak life to the circumstances and not death! Be Blessed!

Proverbs 18:21; Mark 11:22-23

DAILY REFLECTIONS

OCTOBER 17

Morning Prayer

I'm so glad I serve a God I can talk to first thing in the morning! "In the morning, Lord, you hear my voice; in the morning I lay my requests before you and wait expectantly. For you are not a God who is pleased with wickedness; with you, evil people are not welcome. The arrogant cannot stand in your presence. You hate all who do wrong; you destroy those who tell lies. The bloodthirsty and deceitful you, Lord, detest. But I, by your great love, can come into your house; in reverence I bow down toward your holy temple." Be Blessed!

Psalm 5:3-7

DAILY REFLECTIONS

OCTOBER 18

Success

So often people settle for less because they are afraid to step out on faith and go outside of their comfort zone. They may stay in a job they're unhappy in because they don't realize their self-worth and don't have the confidence to look for anything else. Or they stay in a dysfunctional relationship because their self-esteem is so low that they feel no one else would want them. Or they may even be unhappy with themselves but feel powerless to do anything about it. Many people struggle with these kinds of situations every day. However, you serve a God who knows who you are and what you are made of, and even at your lowest point He decided that you were worthy enough to send His Only Begotten Son to die for you! So, if He loved you enough to make that kind of sacrifice, you must be worth saving. Therefore, you must not be afraid to succeed, excel, or conquer whatever comes your way, because "He who began a good work in you will carry it on to completion until the day of Christ Jesus." Be Blessed!

Philippians 1:6

DAILY REFLECTIONS

OCTOBER 19

Provision

I heard a conversation between two people in the store complaining about their jobs. After a period of time, one of them finally said, "At this point, we really should be grateful that we have a job." That is definitely the right attitude to have! We don't know what tomorrow will bring, but one thing is for sure, if you have a job right now you should do your best to keep it. If you don't have one, keep looking and don't give up. Times are hard and a lot of people are looking for work, but if you remain steadfast and determined, something will come through for you. Sitting on the sofa praying for a job is definitely not the answer! The Bible says, "If a man will not work, he shall not eat." We hear that some among you are idle. They are not busy; they are busybodies. Such people we command and urge in the Lord Jesus Christ to settle down and earn the bread they eat." So, get out there and walk in your destiny! Be Blessed!

2 Thessalonians 3:10-12

DAILY REFLECTIONS

OCTOBER 20

Prayer

So many of us only pray when we want or need something from God. However, our prayers should include more than just requests. We can pray to God and praise Him just for being who He is! "I will praise you, O Lord, with all my heart; I will tell of all your wonders. I will be glad and rejoice in you; I will sing praise to your name, O Most High." He is truly worthy of our praise! Be Blessed!

Psalm 9:1-2

DAILY REFLECTIONS

OCTOBER 21

Working in Excellence

Are you committed to seeing a job through to its completion? Do you perform your job in excellence, as if working for the Lord? When God created the heavens and the earth, He created something new every day. However, when it was completed, He could look at His creation and say it was good. Would you be able to say the same? "God saw all that he had made, and it was very good." Be Blessed!

Genesis 1:31

DAILY REFLECTIONS

OCTOBER 22

Rest

Jesus said, "Come to me, all you who are weary and burdened, and I will give you rest. Take my yoke upon you and learn from me, for I am gentle and humble in heart, and you will find rest for your souls." The trials and tribulations of life can easily wear you down if you aren't leaning on the Lord. So, why would you try to go it alone when He's already promised to carry your burden? Begin to take Jesus at His Word and find rest for your soul! Be Blessed!

Matthew 11:28-29

DAILY REFLECTIONS

OCTOBER 23

Protection

People used to say that "God takes care of fools and babies." I don't know where this saying comes from; however, there have been many times in my life where it has proven to be true! Therefore, I thank God for His hedge of protection and His unconditional love in spite of my shortcomings. "He who dwells in the shelter of the Most High will rest in the shadow of the Almighty. I will say of the Lord, "He is my refuge and my fortress, my God, in whom I trust." Be Blessed!

Psalm 91:1-2

DAILY REFLECTIONS

OCTOBER 24

Reciprocity

The cliché "what goes around comes around" was evident in Biblical times and it still stands true today. When you treat people unfairly, you create situations that will eventually cause you to be treated unfairly as well. Conversely, when you treat people right, blessings will chase you down! Therefore, don't spend any more time being unkind to people. You are a child of the Most High God, and people should be able to see God in you whenever they are in your presence. So, "do not let any unwholesome talk come out of your mouths, but only what is helpful for building others up according to their needs, that it may benefit those who listen. And do not grieve the Holy Spirit of God, with whom you were sealed for the day of redemption. Get rid of all bitterness, rage and anger, brawling and slander, along with every form of malice. Be kind and compassionate to one another, forgiving each other, just as in Christ God forgave you." If you do that, I can promise you that you'll be surprised at all of the good things that will come back to you! Be Blessed!

Ephesians 4:29-32

DAILY REFLECTIONS

OCTOBER 25

Our Burden Bearer

Oftentimes, we become weighed down by the cares of life. We worry and fret about how we're going to make it. However, we have a God who stands by willing and eager to carry those burdens for us. "Praise be to the Lord, to God our Savior, who daily bears our burdens."

Psalm 68:19

DAILY REFLECTIONS

OCTOBER 26

Perseverance

Oftentimes when you try something new it may be awkward at first. However, if you keep pressing on, it will become like second nature and it will get easier and easier. But if you give up before you get to that point, you will never find that out. That's what the enemy is counting on. He wants you to give up and stay stuck in your rut. But you are greater than that, and so is the God you serve! "The one who is in you is greater than the one who is in the world." So, determine in your heart to press on, no matter what, and see what great things God has in store for you! Be Blessed!

1 John 4:4

DAILY REFLECTIONS

OCTOBER 27

Integrity

There will be times in your life when your integrity will be tested. The question is how will you respond? God desires that you maintain a posture of integrity at all times. Will you answer His call? "The man of integrity walks securely, but he who takes crooked paths will be found out." Enough said! Be Blessed!

Proverbs 10:9

DAILY REFLECTIONS

OCTOBER 28

Being Still

So often we try to help God fight our battles. However, He doesn't need our help. We just need to get out of His way and let Him do what only He can do. "The Lord will fight for you, you need only to be still." Be Blessed!

Exodus 14:14

DAILY REFLECTIONS

OCTOBER 29

Sacrificial Praise

Oftentimes, we are in the midst of circumstances that require prayer and intercession, but we're so distressed we don't feel like praying. It's during those times that we not only need to pray, but we must also give a sacrificial praise to unleash the deliverance of God. "I will sacrifice a freewill offering to you; I will praise your name, Lord, for it is good. You have delivered me from all my troubles, and my eyes have looked in triumph on my foes." Be Blessed!

Psalm 54:6-7

DAILY REFLECTIONS

OCTOBER 30

Thankfulness

Have you ever found yourself at a loss for words when you've been praying? You don't want to sound repetitious so you find yourself not knowing what to say? Well, I've always been told that praise and worship never gets old! So, whenever you find yourself at a loss for words, just say, "Thanks."

Psalms 100
1. Shout for joy to the Lord, all the earth.
2. Worship the Lord with gladness; come before Him with joyful songs.
3. Know that the Lord is God. It is he who made us, and we are His; we are His people, the sheep of His pasture.
4. Enter His gates with Thankfulness and His courts with praise; give *thanks* to Him and praise His name.
5. For the Lord is good and His love endures forever; His faithfulness continues through all generations.

DAILY REFLECTIONS

OCTOBER 31

Stay in the Race

Several years ago I ran a 10K race in my city; which is about 6.2 miles. As I approached the four-mile marker on Monument Avenue, I started to get really fatigued. Suddenly, the statue of Arthur Ashe caught my eye. I have seen that statue a hundred times, but I never knew there was a scripture inscribed on the bottom of it. The scripture read, "Therefore, since we are surrounded by such a great cloud of witnesses, let us throw off everything that hinders and the sin that so easily entangles, and let us run with perseverance the race marked out for us"! Not only did that give me the extra motivation and energy I needed to finish the race, but it also reminded me of how God knows just what we need, when we need it! "O LORD, you have searched me and you know me. You know when I sit and when I rise; you perceive my thoughts from afar. You discern my going out and my lying down; you are familiar with all my ways. Before a word is on my tongue you know it completely, O LORD." Thank You, God, for your omniscient "all-knowing" power! Be Blessed!!!

Hebrews 12:1, Psalm 139:1–4

DAILY REFLECTIONS

NOVEMBER 1

Perseverance

You will have moments when you will be ready to give up because you don't see any progress or change in your situation. You may even find it hard to believe things will ever change. However, Hebrews 10:35-39 says, "Do not throw away your confidence; it will be richly rewarded. You need to persevere so that when you have done the will of God, you will receive what He has promised. For in just a very little while, "He who is coming will come and will not delay. But my righteous one will live by faith. And if he shrinks back, I will not be pleased with him." But we are not of those who shrink back and are destroyed, but of those who believe and are saved." So, because you are one of His righteous ones, you must persevere and live by faith! Be Blessed!

Hebrews 10:35-39

DAILY REFLECTIONS
___
___
___
___
___
___
___
___
___

NOVEMBER 2

God is For Us

Should we be concerned with whether people like us or not? Should it bother us if someone doesn't want us in their inner circle? What difference does it make if someone likes us or not? Does their affection towards us determine our self-worth or how we feel should feel about ourselves? "If God is for us, who can be against us?" Be Blessed!

Romans 8:31

DAILY REFLECTIONS
_____
_____
_____
_____
_____
_____
_____
_____
_____
_____

NOVEMBER 3

You Have a Friend in Jesus

Do you have any "ride or die" friends that will stick with you, no matter what? We all need at least ONE friend like that. However, if you don't, know that you have a friend like that in Jesus. He is a "friend who sticks closer than any brother." "Who will rise up for me against the wicked? Who will take a stand for me against evildoers? Unless the Lord had given me help, I would soon have dwelt in the silence of death. When I said, "My foot is slipping," your unfailing love, Lord, supported me. When anxiety was great within me, your consolation brought me joy." Thank You, Lord, for being my "ride or die"! Be Blessed!

Proverbs 18:24, Psalm 94:16-19

DAILY REFLECTIONS

NOVEMBER 4

Listening to God

I've often heard people say, "if you want to make God laugh, tell Him your plans for your life." That's exactly what a lot of us do when we pray. We tell God what we want, but don't wait to listen to what His plans are for our lives. We give Him a laundry list of prayer requests, without ever stopping to "be still." God doesn't need our lists. He knows what our needs are before we even ask. "You have searched me, Lord, and you know me. You know when I sit and when I rise; you perceive my thoughts from afar. You discern my going out and my lying down; you are familiar with all my ways. Before a word is on my tongue you, Lord, know it completely." So, it's OK for you to go to Him with your prayer requests, but then be willing to just sit with Him a minute and listen. Be Blessed!

Psalm 139:1-4

DAILY REFLECTIONS

NOVEMBER 5

Humbleness

Don't you hate it when people are boastful? No one wants to sit around and hear someone talk about themselves all the time. God even knew about "boastful people," and made provision to keep them humble and in place! "For it is by grace you have been saved, through faith—and this is not from yourselves, it is the gift of God— not by works, so that no one can boast." Therefore, let us receive God's gift of grace humbly, and not think more highly of ourselves than we ought to! Be Blessed!

Ephesians 2:8-9

DAILY REFLECTIONS
___
___
___
___
___
___
___
___

NOVEMBER 6

Rejoice in The Lord

You can mope around and have a pity party because of the things that have happened to you in your life. Or, you can choose to rejoice because you survived it, and are still alive to talk about it. The choice is up to you, however, I made the choice to rejoice! "Rejoice in the Lord always. I will say it again: Rejoice!" Be Blessed!

Philippians 4:4

DAILY REFLECTIONS

NOVEMBER 7

Courage

Many of us go through life not taking advantage of opportunities that are before us. Why is that? Is it because of fear? Or is it because our expectations are too low? Whatever the reason, we must renew our minds to think bigger! We serve a God who knows no boundaries because "nothing is too hard for Him." Therefore, we do not have to be afraid to enlarge our territory and ask God for what we want. As Children of the Most High God, we must realize that "we are more than conquerors through Him that loved us." Be Blessed!

Jeremiah 32:17, 1 Chronicles 4:10, Romans 8:37

DAILY REFLECTIONS

NOVEMBER 8

Omniscience

A lot of people try to cover up their feelings and develop a "poker face" in the toughest situations! However, God is not fooled by your facades. He knows your innermost being. He knows what you are thinking, feeling, and doing at any given moment. "O Lord, you have searched me and you know me. You know when I sit and when I rise; you perceive my thoughts from afar. You discern my going out and my lying down; you are familiar with all my ways." Therefore, it is useless to try to keep your true feelings from God, even if some of the feelings are directed towards Him! God already knows your thoughts, so you might as well confess them, so He can help you move past them. It is even normal to be angry at God sometimes. The Bible says even Jesus got angry, and at times, even questioned God. But after all was said and done, His response was always, "nevertheless, Thy Will Be Done." Therefore, you must learn to put your trust in God because He is the one who will never let you down! Be Blessed!

Psalm 139:1-4, Matthew 26:42

DAILY REFLECTIONS

NOVEMBER 9

Praise

There are times when circumstances put us in a spirit of praise, and then there are times when we have to give a sacrifice of praise. Whatever the situation, though, it's just a wonderful thing to give God praise! "Shout for joy to the Lord, all the earth. Worship the Lord with gladness; come before Him with joyful songs. Know that the Lord is God. It is He who made us, and we are His; we are His people, the sheep of His pasture. Enter His gates with Thankfulness and His courts with praise; give thanks to Him and praise His name. For the Lord is good and His love endures forever; His faithfulness continues through all generations." Be Blessed!

Psalm 100

DAILY REFLECTIONS

NOVEMBER 10

Love

Letting go of past mistakes is one of the hardest things we will ever have to do. It is difficult because we tend to be harder on ourselves than we are on anybody else. As a result, it is extremely difficult to forgive ourselves for the mistakes we've made in the past. However, we have all made bad choices and decisions at one time or another. But we often put unfair and unrealistic expectations of perfection on ourselves. Therefore, when we fall short and have to face the fact that we are not perfect, most of us have a hard time dealing with that. God loves us unconditionally; faults and all and we must learn to love ourselves in the same manner. When we begin to love ourselves as God loves us, we no longer have to prove ourselves to others or to ourselves. We can be happy with who we are, even with our imperfections! Love is patient, love is kind. It does not envy, it does not boast, it is not proud. It is not rude, it is not self-seeking, it is not easily angered, it keeps no record of wrongs. Love does not delight in evil but rejoices with the truth. It always protects, always trusts, always hopes, always perseveres. Love never fails." Be Blessed!

1 Corinthians 13:4-8.

DAILY REFLECTIONS

NOVEMBER 11

Truthfulness

True honesty is one of the hardest things in life to achieve. It is difficult because we are taught at an early age to mask our "true" feelings and pretend that everything is alright no matter what is going on with us. As we grow older, it only gets worse. We are told things like, "never let them see you cry," "it's all good, just shake it off," "learn to roll with the punches," "put on your poker face," etc. The problem is, we're never really told how to deal with the disappointments we encounter in life, and if we lie to ourselves long enough we won't know how to be honest with ourselves even when we really need to! However, we must remember that "The Lord detests lying lips, but He delights in men who are truthful." So, let's follow the Lord's example and learn to be truthful to ourselves and to everyone else! Be Blessed!

Proverbs 12:22

DAILY REFLECTIONS

NOVEMBER 12

Provision

We live in a society where everybody tries to outdo each other. It is called, 'keeping up with the Jones.' The problem with that philosophy is that it has caused a lot of people to go into debt trying to impress others. God provides for us daily and He does not want us to go into debt because we are living beyond our means. When we esteem ourselves in God, we will not have to compare what we have to what others have because we will be content with how God has blessed us. Therefore, "keep your lives free from the love of money and be content with what you have, because God has said, "Never will I leave you; never will I forsake you." So we say with confidence, "The Lord is my helper; I will not be afraid. What can man do to me? Be Blessed!

Hebrews 13:5-6

DAILY REFLECTIONS

NOVEMBER 13

Joy

Laughter is good for the soul and has even been linked to general good health and well-being. We know God is the one who ultimately heals us, of course, but it only makes God's job easier if we're already joyous and happy people. "When the Lord brought back the captives to Zion, we were like men who dreamed. Our mouths were filled with laughter, our tongues with songs of joy. Then it was said among the nations, "The Lord has done great things for them." The Lord has done great things for us, and we are filled with joy. Restore our fortunes, O Lord, like streams in the Negev. Those who sow in tears will reap with songs of joy. He who goes out weeping, carrying seed to sow, will return with songs of joy, carrying sheaves with him." So, even if we don't think we have anything to laugh about, we must remember that God is able to turn our weeping into gladness! "Rejoice in the Lord always." Be Blessed!

Psalm 126:1-6, Philippians 4:4

DAILY REFLECTIONS

NOVEMBER 14

Motivation

We all have days where we lack motivation and drive. The cares of the world can wear us down and we become tired and full of despair. It was during those times that David "had to encourage himself in the Lord." We must learn how to do that as well. But if we find we don't even have the strength to do that, then that's the time to call on God and His mighty power. We must not falsely believe we have to do everything by ourselves. God is always there to catch us when we stumble, and lift us up when we are down. "If the Lord delights in a man's way, He makes his steps firm; though he stumble, he will not fall, for the Lord upholds him with His hand." So, always remember God will be there when you call. Be Blessed!

1 Samuel 30:6, Psalm 37:23-24

DAILY REFLECTIONS

NOVEMBER 15

Discipleship

Have you ever heard the expression "you're so heavenly bound that you're no earthly good?" It's describing people who spend so much time "preaching down" to people that they don't even realize they're not able to win them over like that. If you are trying to reach out to someone to encourage them to turn their life over to Christ, you must be willing to meet them wherever *they* are, not where *you* are. If you start "bible beating" them or start quoting a bunch of scriptures at them, you will probably run them away or turn them off. That's because you're probably talking over their head, or beyond their current comprehension. Therefore, you must be able to talk with them in a language and on a level they can understand. Most of the time when people use their knowledge of the Bible as a way to impress people, it is usually because they are trying to make themselves feel more important. However, "pride goes before destruction, a haughty spirit before a fall." So, the next time you want to minister to someone and bring them to Christ, just keep it simple and tell them all about what the Lord has done for you! Be Blessed!

Proverbs 16:18-19

DAILY REFLECTIONS

NOVEMBER 16

Perseverance

When you start an exercise program, you will experience a burning sensation when you begin to stress the muscle. Although it may be a little uncomfortable at first, you must try to push through it because as you continue to put stress on the muscle, it will grow and become stronger. God does the same thing with you when He is maturing you. You may get frustrated or upset when trials and tribulations come your way. However, just remember it is only God putting "stress" on you in order to make you stronger. "Consider it pure joy, my brothers, whenever you face trials of many kinds, because you know that the testing of your faith develops perseverance. Perseverance must finish its work so that you may be mature and complete, not lacking anything." Be Blessed!

James 1:2-4

DAILY REFLECTIONS

NOVEMBER 17

Faith in God Results in Indescribable Peace

Oftentimes you get upset or stressed out because you're assuming the worst will happen. But whenever you're in doubt, instead of thinking the worst, think positively. No matter what the circumstances, "nothing is too hard for God" to handle. So, instead of worrying about it, put your faith in God and know that He will work it out Do not be anxious about anything, but in every situation, by prayer and petition, with thanksgiving, present your requests to God. And the peace of God, which transcends all understanding, will guard your hearts and your minds in Christ Jesus." Be Blessed!

Jeremiah 32:17, Philippians 4:6-7

DAILY REFLECTIONS

NOVEMBER 18

Redemption

Oftentimes, people wonder if the "still small voice" they hear at times is God. One thing I know for sure, He sent His only Son to die for us so that we may have the gift of eternal life! He said, "I am the good shepherd; I know my sheep and my sheep know me—just as the Father knows me and I know the Father—and I lay down my life for the sheep." Be Blessed!

John 10:14-15

DAILY REFLECTIONS

NOVEMBER 19

Forgiveness

When we withhold forgiveness in our hearts, it eventually turns into resentment. Meanwhile, the people we are harboring the resentment against usually have no idea we are even offended. So, if we can look beyond the offense and look instead at the person, we can hopefully forgive them just as Christ forgave us. None of us are perfect, and while we are on this journey together we will fall short from time to time. However, as children of the Most High God, we must be willing to forgive, even if it means doing so again and again and again. Once we do, the healing process can begin. "Then Peter came to Jesus and asked, "Lord, how many times shall I forgive my brother when he sins against me? Up to seven times?" Jesus answered, "I tell you, not seven times, but seventy-seven times." Be Blessed!

Matthew 18:21-22

DAILY REFLECTIONS

NOVEMBER 20

More Than A Conqueror

Things can happen in life that may cause your self-esteem and self-worth to be affected. For instance, you could lose your job, have a change in your health, be in an accident, get divorced, gain or lose weight, lose a loved one, or any number of things. However, as a child of God, you don't have to be affected in that way if something happens. You serve a God who is able to see you through any circumstance. So, even if one or all of those things happen to you, you can still hold your head up high knowing that "you are more than a conqueror through Him." Be Blessed!

Romans 8:37

DAILY REFLECTIONS

NOVEMBER 21

Harmony

If you work outside the home, you will spend most of your day with the people you work with. Therefore, it is in your best interest (and theirs) to have a good relationship with them. You don't have to like them, but as Christians, you do have to love them! I realize this is not always easy to do, however, harboring anger and resentment towards them isn't the answer either.

> "Live in harmony with one another. Do not be proud but be willing to associate with people of low position. Do not be conceited. Do not repay anyone evil for evil. Be careful to do what is right in the eyes of everybody. If it is possible, as far as it depends on you, live at peace with everyone." This is the good and perfect will of God! Be Blessed!
>
> Romans 12:16-18

DAILY REFLECTIONS

NOVEMBER 22

Love

If God were to tear down that wall you've been hiding behind, what would He find? Would it be fear, a false sense of pride, arrogance, or insecurity? Or would it be love, peace, and joy? God desires for you to have that love, peace, and joy, but all too often you are so busy hiding behind the wall that you can't enjoy the life that Jesus died to give you. Isn't it time you came out from behind that wall and lived your life to the fullest? Jesus came so that you "may have life, and have it to the full." Be Blessed!

John 10:10

DAILY REFLECTIONS

NOVEMBER 23

Forgiveness

Most of us know that we have to forgive; however, the problem is we don't know how to do it! How do we move from hurt to forgiveness? The first thing is to stop focusing on what happened. It is impossible to move forward if we keep rehearsing the situation over and over again. Instead, we must focus on the positive things and train ourselves to think the best instead of the worst. "For if you forgive other people when they sin against you, your heavenly Father will also forgive you. Be Blessed!

Philippians 4:8

DAILY REFLECTIONS

_____
_____
_____
_____
_____
_____
_____
_____
_____
_____

NOVEMBER 24

Compassion

So often people forget what they did before they became saved and how graciously God delivered them. Instead of being grateful, some even become arrogant and indignant and have the audacity to stand in judgment of others! However, God's word says that "for by the grace given me I say to every one of you: Do not think of yourself more highly than you ought, but rather think of yourself with sober judgment, in accordance with the measure of faith God has given you." Therefore, have compassion on your fellow man because it was not that long ago that God had to exercise compassion with you! Be Blessed!

Romans 12:3

DAILY REFLECTIONS

NOVEMBER 25

Temptation

What do you do when you lose the motivation to be disciplined? One of the key components of any 12-step program (i.e., Alcoholics Anonymous) is to partner with a sponsor. A sponsor is suggested because the founder realized that there would be times of temptation, and the sponsor's role is to talk you through that trying time. During your walk with God, you, too, will be tempted. It is during those times that you must call on your "spiritual sponsor"; the "Wonderful Counselor, Mighty God, Everlasting Father, and Prince of Peace." "No temptation has seized you except what is common to man. And God is faithful; He will not let you be tempted beyond what you can bear. But when you are tempted, He will also provide a way out so that you can stand up under it." Be Blessed!

Isaiah 9:6, 1 Corinthians 10:13

DAILY REFLECTIONS

NOVEMBER 26

Humility

If you asked people you know to write down several adjectives to describe you, would they be able to say anything good about you? Would you be surprised if all of the words were not positive? Well, the truth is, no one is perfect, so you should expect there to be some flaws in your character. The question is what are you going to do about them? You can sit around and feel bad about them, or you can open your heart and your mind and allow God to change those ways that are not indicative of whom He created you to be. "Search me, O God, and know my heart; test me and know my anxious thoughts. See if there is any offensive way in me, and lead me in the way everlasting." God created you as a masterpiece and He can finish what He started! Be Blessed!

Psalm 139:23-24

DAILY REFLECTIONS

NOVEMBER 27

Faith

Sometimes things will happen that will totally blindside us. It's during those times that we must hold onto every ounce of faith we have. Walking in faith is not easy because it requires us to believe in something we can't see yet. It's not hard to believe in something we already see is happening. But blind faith means believing in something even when it looks like it's *not* going to happen! "Now faith is being sure of what we hope for and certain of what we do not see." So, continue to walk on in faith, knowing that God will always honor His promises and will do just what He said! Be Blessed!

Hebrews 11:6

DAILY REFLECTIONS

NOVEMBER 28

Encouraging Friends

The cliché "birds of a feather flock together" means that we will be like those we hang around. Therefore, if you want to be successful in life, don't hang out with people who have no ambition. It's not easy trying to reach your dreams, and the last thing you need to do is hang out with people who are "dream killers." Instead, you need to surround yourself with people who have vision and are passionate about fulfilling their dreams, too. If you do that, during those times when things get tough, you will have a network of people who will encourage you and support you because they believe in your dream, too. "A friend loves at all times." "If one falls down, his friend can help him up. But pity the man who falls and has no one to help him up!" Be Blessed!

Proverbs 17:17, Ecclesiastes 4:10

DAILY REFLECTIONS

NOVEMBER 29

Perseverance

Have you ever been at a point in your life when you felt stuck in a rut? That no matter what you did, you didn't seem to be making any progress? Well, don't let the enemy deceive you. He will try to discourage you so that you will give up before you get your breakthrough. But Jesus did not sacrifice His life for you only to have you give up and throw in the towel. So, no matter how long it takes or how hard it gets, keep pressing on because "at the proper time you will reap a harvest if you don't give up." Be Blessed!

Galatians 6:9

DAILY REFLECTIONS

NOVEMBER 30

Patience

It's not easy waiting on the Lord. Most of us want things when we want them, and waiting is not on our agenda! However, we must be thankful that God is just saying wait because He could have said *no*. There are many reasons why God may make us wait. We aren't all-knowing like God is, so we won't always understand what He is doing. We can, however, trust Him to do what He knows is best. We may think we know what's best, but the truth is, we don't. So, as we learn to wait on God, we will find out that He knows what He is doing, and we can trust Him to work things out for our good. "And we know that in all things God works for the good of those who love Him, who have been called according to His purpose." Be Blessed!

Romans 8:28

DAILY REFLECTIONS

DECEMBER 1

Strongholds

Old habits die hard! However, in order to make a difference in the world, you have to be willing to break old habits by any means necessary! It has been said that you have to do something 21 times in order for it to become a habit. So, why not reverse that and say you have to <u>stop</u> doing something 21 times in order for the habit to be broken! You may have a difficult habit to break and you've been trying to do it for quite some time. But don't give up! "You can do all things through Christ who strengthens you." Be Blessed!

Philippians 4:13

DAILY REFLECTIONS

DECEMBER 2

Prayer

When you pray, what do you pray for? Do you pray for God's best or do you settle for what you think you deserve? No one deserves the blessings of God. However, because of His mercy and grace, He desires to bless you anyway. Therefore, ask boldly for the things that you want and need, believing that God "is able to do exceeding abundantly above anything that you could ever ask or imagine." Jabez boldly asked God to bless him indeed and God answered his prayer. "Jabez cried out to the God of Israel, "Oh, that you would bless me and enlarge my territory! Let your hand be with me, and keep me from harm so that I will be free from pain." And God granted his request." If God could bless someone whose name meant "trouble and pain," just think what He will be able to do for you! "You have not, because you ask not." Be Blessed!

Ephesians 3:20, 1 Chronicles 4:10, James 4:2

DAILY REFLECTIONS

DECEMBER 3

Courage

How do you find the courage to move on when you're sick and tired of being sick and tired?

Well, the first thing is to stop focusing on your situation. If you constantly dwell on your circumstances, you will remain stuck there. In order to rise above your circumstances, you must renew your mind and start focusing on where you want to be instead of where you currently are. You have to be able to see it in order to believe it! "Have faith in God," Jesus answered. "I tell you the truth, if anyone says to this mountain, 'Go, throw yourself into the sea,' and does not doubt in his heart but believes that what he says will happen, it will be done for him. Therefore I tell you, whatever you ask for in prayer, believe that you have received it, and it will be yours." Be Blessed!

Mark 11:22-24

DAILY REFLECTIONS

DECEMBER 4

God's Provision

Oftentimes when we least expect it, something that we've been praying for suddenly comes to pass. It will happen so miraculously that we can't help but give God the credit. Some may believe they always give God the glory for the things that happen to them. But if we are truly honest with ourselves we know that isn't always the case. We often fool ourselves into believing the enemy's lies telling us that we pulled our own selves up by our bootstraps and we alone worked hard to get the things we have. But God is the only one worthy of praise. Some of us have become too prideful and arrogant and we must change those ways before it causes us to fall. "Pride goes before destruction, a haughty spirit before a fall. It is better to be lowly in spirit and among the oppressed than to share plunder with the proud." So, remember even though we have worked hard to get where we are, it is God "who brings the increase"; not us! Be Blessed!

Proverbs 16:18-19, 1 Corinthians 3:6

DAILY REFLECTIONS

DECEMBER 5

God's Representative

Are you a representative of God wherever you go? Are you a representative at work? At home with your family? Or just at church when you think the pastor is looking? God is everywhere and He knows everything. So, there's no use pretending to be something you're not because He knows the real you that nobody else sees. "Follow God's example, therefore, as dearly loved children and walk in the way of love." So, always remember that and be are a representative of God wherever you are! Be Blessed!

Ephesians 5:1

DAILY REFLECTIONS

DECEMBER 6

Faithfulness

It is a wonderful thing to be able to trust a God who is faithful to His word. So many times in our dealings with people, we are often let down because they don't keep their word. When they do this, it is difficult to trust anything they say in the future. Fortunately, we don't have to worry about that with God because He always remains true to His word! "God is not a man, that He should lie, nor a son of man, that He should change His mind. Does He speak and then not act? Does He promise and not fulfill?" "So is my word that goes out from my mouth: It will not return to me empty, but will accomplish what I desire and achieve the purpose for which I sent it." Thank you, Lord, for being a man of your word! Be Blessed!

Numbers 23:19, Isaiah 55:11

DAILY REFLECTIONS

DECEMBER 7

Enemy's Attacks

There will be times when you feel as if you're under attack. It's during those times that you must remind yourself, "If anyone does attack you, it will not be my doing; whoever attacks you will surrender to you. "See, it is I who created the blacksmith who fans the coals into flame and forges a weapon fit for its work. And it is I who have created the destroyer to work havoc; no weapon forged against you will prevail, and you will refute every tongue that accuses you. This is the heritage of the servants of the Lord, and this is their vindication from me," declares the Lord." Be Blessed!

Isaiah 54:15-17

DAILY REFLECTIONS

DECEMBER 8

Blessings

Oftentimes we hear people pray, "Lord, thank you for waking me up in my right mind." We usually don't understand or appreciate what that means until we've seen someone go through something devastating, such as dementia, where their memory deteriorates over time. But we shouldn't have to wait for something like that to happen before we realize how blessed we are. It is a blessing just to have activity of our limbs and a reasonable portion of health and strength. So, even if we aren't where we want to be, at least we're not where we used to be, or where we could be! "Praise be to the God and Father of our Lord Jesus Christ, who has blessed us in the heavenly realms with every spiritual blessing in Christ." Be Blessed!

Ephesians 1:3

DAILY REFLECTIONS

DECEMBER 9

Anxiety

Circumstances that are supposed to bring the most joy in your life often cause you the most stress. Things like a new job, a new house, a new baby, etc. All of these things are blessings from God, but the anxiety each of them brings is very real. If you can remember who brought the blessing, however, you will realize He is able to do all things. "Humble yourselves, therefore, under God's mighty hand, that He may lift you up in due time. Cast all your anxiety on Him because He cares for you. Be Blessed!

1 Peter 5:6-7

DAILY REFLECTIONS

DECEMBER 10

Doubt

After all of the things God has done in our lives, why do we still doubt Him? If we're not careful, we will be just like the Israelites who walked around the same mountain for 40 years. God brought them out of one trial after another, yet they still doubted! Even though life may throw us some curve balls every now and then, we can allow God to raise us above our circumstances. "God is our refuge and strength, an ever-present help in trouble. Therefore we will not fear, though the earth give way and the mountains fall into the heart of the sea, though its waters roar and foam and the mountains quake with their surging. There is a river whose streams make glad the city of God, the holy place where the Most High dwells. God is within her, she will not fall; God will help her at break of day. Therefore, you can "be still and know that He is God." Be Blessed!

Psalm 46:1-5, 10

DAILY REFLECTIONS

DECEMBER 11

Favor

Have you ever tried to live your life without God in it? So many people attempt it because they think the grass is greener on the other side. They look at others and compare their lives to theirs. However, no one really knows what goes on in the life of someone behind closed doors. Things can appear one way on the outside but be totally different on the inside. So, you must try to hold onto the knowledge that "God is no respecter of persons" and what He does for others, He can do for you, too! "I now realize how true it is that God does not show favoritism but accepts men from every nation who fear Him and do what is right. Be Blessed!

Acts 10:34-35

DAILY REFLECTIONS

DECEMBER 12

Patience

Have you ever noticed when you have a deadline to meet, time flies by extremely fast; but when you're waiting on something it seems to take forever? I don't know why it happens like that, but it sure can be frustrating! The best thing is to learn how to wait with a good attitude, and that is definitely not easy! David gave instructions in Psalm 27 when he said, "Wait patiently for the Lord. Be brave and courageous. Yes, wait patiently for the Lord." So, the key to having a good attitude while you are waiting is to learn patience! Be Blessed!

Psalm 27:14

DAILY REFLECTIONS

DECEMBER 13

Generosity

Generosity is something a lot of people struggle with. They are afraid to be generous because they are afraid of being taken advantage of. It is a sad day when people have to be afraid to be nice! However, when you give with the love of Christ as your motive, God will work it out for your good, even if the intended person means to do ill will with it. When you give from a humble and broken spirit, you will get back what you gave and more abundantly. "Give, and it will be given to you. A good measure, pressed down, shaken together and running over, will be poured into your lap. For with the measure you use, it will be measured to you." Be Blessed!

Luke 6:38

DAILY REFLECTIONS

DECEMBER 14

Discipline

Why is it so hard for us to be disciplined with our bodies? Even though we know our bodies are the temple of the Holy Spirit, we don't always treat them that way. We eat what we want, even when we know it's not good for us. Or we stop exercising because we just don't feel like doing it. When we do this, however, it is indicative of a rebellious spirit. In order to overcome rebellious behaviors, we must first acknowledge and admit it; and then pray and ask God to deliver us so we can do what is pleasing in His sight. "Therefore, I urge you, brothers and sisters, in view of God's mercy, to offer your bodies as a living sacrifice, holy and pleasing to God—this is your true and proper worship." Be Blessed!

Romans 12:1

DAILY REFLECTIONS

DECEMBER 15

Protection

So many times we get in situations we feel we can't get out of. However, God will come to our rescue if we call out to Him. "He reached down from on high and took hold of me; He drew me out of deep waters. He rescued me from my powerful enemy, from my foes, who were too strong for me. They confronted me in the day of my disaster, but the Lord was my support. He brought me out into a spacious place; He rescued me because He delighted in me." There is always a way out when we put God at the center of our lives! Be Blessed!

Psalm 18:16-19

DAILY REFLECTIONS

DECEMBER 16

Determination

Whenever God is ready to take you to the next level, the adversary will rear his ugly head. So, don't expect him to make things easy for you. He is determined to keep you from getting where God is trying to take you. However, you must be even more determined to reach the level God has destined for you! It may seem impossible when you look at your circumstances. But if God is orchestrating your future, you can rest assured He will empower you to overcome any obstacles. "Therefore, my dear brothers and sisters, stand firm. Let nothing move you. Always give yourselves fully to the work of the Lord, because you know that your labor in the Lord is not in vain. "Be Blessed!

1 Corinthians 15:58

DAILY REFLECTIONS

DECEMBER 17

Understanding

There will be times in our lives when things will happen that we don't understand. It's how we handle those times that will make all the difference in the world. Knowledge is power, but we will never gain knowledge if we don't ask questions when we don't understand something. God doesn't mind when we ask Him questions because our questions indicate that we desire to have honest and open communication with Him. "For the Lord gives wisdom, and from His mouth come knowledge and understanding. He holds victory in store for the upright, He is a shield to those whose walk is blameless, for He guards the course of the just and protects the way of His faithful ones. Then you will understand what is right and just and fair—every good path. For wisdom will enter your heart, and knowledge will be pleasant to your soul." Be Blessed!

Proverbs 2:6-10

DAILY REFLECTIONS

DECEMBER 18

New Beginning

One thing is sure, as long as you live on this earth, things will change. If you're a person who doesn't like change and has a hard time dealing with it, then you need to make an attitude adjustment. Things are going to change whether you like it or not, so you might as well get used to it and learn to adjust. In the Old Testament, God gave Lot and his family a chance to start anew. However, Lot's wife had a hard time leaving the past behind and moving forward to something new. She looked back at the city as it was being destroyed (even though God had told them not to), and she was turned into a pillar of salt. How many of you are walking "pillars of salt" because you are holding onto the past when God is trying to change you? Let go of your fears, anxieties, and stubbornness about the unknown and embrace the future and all of the changes that come with it! God is trying to do a new thing in you, so will you let go of the past so He can do it? Be Blessed!

Genesis 19:15-26

DAILY REFLECTIONS

DECEMBER 19

Purpose

It is so easy to get distracted from what God has called us to do. We get caught up in the stresses of life and forget that we were put here for a purpose and whatever God has called us to do, He will give us the ability to do! "And He made known to us the mystery of His will according to His good pleasure, which He purposed in Christ, to be put into effect when the times will have reached their fulfillment—to bring all things in heaven and on earth together under one head, even Christ. In Him we were also chosen, having been predestined according to the plan of Him who works out everything in conformity with the purpose of His will, in order that we, who were the first to hope in Christ, might be for the praise of His glory." Be Blessed!

Ephesians 1:9-12

DAILY REFLECTIONS

DECEMBER 20

Guidance

Have you ever been at a place in your life when you didn't know which way to turn? Things were happening all around you, but you just couldn't figure out what to do? Well, join the club! Everyone has been at that place at one time or another. As a child of God, however, you don't have to try to figure out what to do. You can go to God and seek His guidance. He is the one who created you, and He knows what is best for you. So, don't lose another night's sleep trying to figure out your circumstances. Take it to God and leave it there! "Trust in the Lord with all your heart and lean not on your own understanding; in all your ways acknowledge Him, and He will make your paths straight." Be Blessed!

Proverbs 3:5-6

DAILY REFLECTIONS

DECEMBER 21

Faith

Sometimes things will happen that appear to be the worst thing in the world. However, as life goes on, it may turn out to be a blessing in disguise. For instance, you may lose a job, which would appear to be terrible thing. However, God may use that circumstance to place you in another job that is much better than the one you lost! Or it could be the spring board to launch you into your own business that you have been talking about starting for a long time but have been dragging your feet getting it started. You won't always understand what God is doing while you're in the midst of the situation. But if you hold on and keep the faith, all things will be revealed in time. "For we walk by faith and not by sight." Be Blessed!

2 Corinthians 5:7

DAILY REFLECTIONS

DECEMBER 22

Anxieties

The news can be full of distressing current events, as well as warnings of potential weather disturbances. However, no matter how bad things look, we still can't allow them to cause us anxiety. Even in the worst situations, God is still in control and able to see us through. "Do not be anxious about anything, but in everything, by prayer and petition, with Thankfulness, present your requests to God. And the peace of God, which transcends all understanding, will guard your hearts and your minds in Christ Jesus." Be Blessed!

Philippians 4:6-7

DAILY REFLECTIONS

DECEMBER 23

Trustworthy

Verizon Wireless prides itself on being the "most reliable network." They claim to be more reliable than Sprint, AT&T, and any other network. But who can you depend on to be reliable when you need spiritual fulfillment? God and God Alone! "The Lord Himself goes before you and will be with you; He will never leave you nor forsake you. Do not be afraid; do not be discouraged." You can count on Him now and forever more! Be Blessed!

Deuteronomy 31:8

DAILY REFLECTIONS

DECEMBER 24

Positive vs. Negative

There are always two ways to look at a situation; positively or negatively. For example, if someone loses their job, they could look at it negatively and wonder how they're going to pay their bills or meet their obligations. Or, they could look at it as an opportunity to get a better paying job doing something they are really passionate about. Most people, unfortunately, view things from a negative standpoint because they allow fear to set in and cloud their judgment. But when you're a child of the Most High God, you don't have to be afraid! God is in control and able to do "immeasurably more than you can ask or imagine." "Do not be afraid. Stand firm and you will see the deliverance the Lord will bring you today." Be Blessed!

Exodus 14:13

DAILY REFLECTIONS

DECEMBER 25

Christmas

" For unto us a child is born, unto us a son is given: and the government shall be upon his shoulder: and His name shall be called Wonderful, Counsellor, The mighty God, The everlasting Father, The Prince of Peace." What a wonderful way for God to show His love for us; by sending a Savior to redeem us from all of our sins! What a Mighty God we serve. Thank you, Lord, for sending your Son, Jesus Christ, so that we might be saved! Be Blessed!

Isaiah 9:6

DAILY REFLECTIONS

DECEMBER 26

Don't Forget

We must never forget where our blessings come from. A lot of people forget about God when things are going good. But let something bad happen and they're talking to God 24 hours a day! The Israelites were quick to forget the miraculous things God did for them while they were in the wilderness. They even started worshipping idol gods! However, we don't have to make the same mistakes they did. We can stay on the straight and narrow path and allow God to lead us along the way. Jesus declared that "I am the way, the truth and the life." So, we can't go wrong if we follow Him! Be Blessed!

John 14:6

DAILY REFLECTIONS

DECEMBER 27

Trusting God

In a time where it's so hard to trust people, it is so comforting to know we serve a God who we can trust wholeheartedly. "The Lord is a refuge for the oppressed, a stronghold in times of trouble. Those who know your name will trust in you, for you, Lord, have never forsaken those who seek you." Thank you, Lord, for being a God we can trust! Be Blessed!

Psalm 9:9-10

DAILY REFLECTIONS

_____
_____
_____
_____
_____
_____
_____
_____
_____
_____

DECEMBER 28

Accomplishment

Your outlook on life determines how far you will go. If you set your standards low, then you won't have far to go to reach them. On the other hand, if you set high expectations, you will work harder and feel a much greater sense of accomplishment when you achieve your goals. Therefore, set high expectations and "press toward the mark for the prize of the high calling of God in Christ Jesus." Be Blessed!

Philippians 3:14

DAILY REFLECTIONS

DECEMBER 29

Rest

Sometimes when you go through tough times, you try to travel the road alone. However, it is not necessary to do that. God is there willing and able to carry the load for you. Jesus said, "Come to me, all you who are weary and burdened, and I will give you rest. Take my yoke upon you and learn from me, for I am gentle and humble in heart, and you will find rest for your souls. For my yoke is easy and my burden is light." Be Blessed!

Matthew 11:28-30

DAILY REFLECTIONS

DECEMBER 30

Repentance

When you close your eyes at night, what kind of thoughts cross your mind? Can you go to bed with a clear conscience knowing that you have not wronged anyone intentionally? If not, do you go to God with a spirit of repentance or do you arrogantly try to act as if you've done nothing wrong? God knows your heart and He knows your true intent. So, if you go to Him and confess your sins, He is faithful and just to forgive. "If we claim to be without sin, we deceive ourselves and the truth is not in us. If we confess our sins, He is faithful and just and will forgive us our sins and purify us from all unrighteousness. If we claim we have not sinned, we make Him out to be a liar and His word has no place in our lives." Therefore, confess your sins to God, so you may be forgiven! Be Blessed!

1 John 1:8-10

DAILY REFLECTIONS

DECEMBER 31

Pride

Pride and fear often go hand in hand. Most prideful people are really just hiding behind their fears. They display a false sense of pride to camouflage their true feelings. However, as children of the Most High God, we don't have to be prideful or fearful. Because of God's protection and His unconditional love, we can be assured He has our best interest at heart and will work things out for our good. "If the Lord delights in a man's way, He makes his steps firm; though he stumble, he will not fall, for the Lord upholds him with His hand. I was young and now I am old, yet I have never seen the righteous forsaken or their children begging bread." Be Blessed!

Psalm 37:23-25

DAILY REFLECTIONS